SELF-ACCEPTANCE

SELF-ACCEPTANCE

The Key to Recovery from Mental Illness

A Self-Help Workbook to Assist
Mental-Health-Services Consumers
Recovering from Schizophrenia,
Bipolar Disorder, or Major Depression

Victor Ashear

with

Vanessa Hastings

CENTRAL RECOVERY PRESS

LAS VEGAS

Central Recovery Press (CRP) is committed to publishing exceptional materials addressing addiction treatment, recovery, and behavioral healthcare topics, including original and quality books, audio/visual communications, and web-based new media. Through a diverse selection of titles, we seek to contribute a broad range of unique resources for professionals, recovering individuals and their families, and the general public.

For more information, visit www.centralrecoverypress.com.

Publisher: Central Recovery Press
            3321 N. Buffalo Drive
            Las Vegas, NV 89129

20 19 18 17 16 15   1 2 3 4 5

ISBN: 978-1-937612-91-7 (paper)
       978-1-937612-92-4 (e-book)

"I Am Me" from *Self-Esteem* by Virginia M. Satir. Copyright © 1970, 1975, 2001 by Virginia Satir. Used by permission of Celestial Arts, an imprint of the Crown Publishing Group, a division of Penguin Random House LLC. All rights reserved.

"How I Perceive and Manage My Illness" by Esso Leete. Reprinted with permission from Schizophrenia Bulletin.

Photo of Victor Ashear by Janet Ashear. Used with permission.
Photo of Vanessa Hastings by Marcy Dorsey. Used with permission.

Publisher's Note: This book contains general information about how acceptance of the self and the effects of mental illness can help facilitate recovery from schizophrenia, bipolar disorder, or major depression. The information is not medical advice and should not be treated as such.

Central Recovery Press makes no representations or warranties in relation to the medical information in this book; this book is not an alternative to medical advice from your doctor or other professional healthcare provider. If you have any specific questions about any medical matter you should consult your doctor or other professional healthcare provider. If you think you or someone close to you may be suffering from any medical condition, you should seek immediate medical attention. You should never delay seeking medical advice, disregard medical advice, or discontinue medical treatment because of information in this or any book.

Central Recovery Press books represent the experiences of their authors only. Every effort has been made to ensure that events, institutions, and statistics presented in our books as facts are accurate and up-to-date.

Cover design by David Hardy
Interior design by Deb Tremper, Six Penny Graphics

"The feeling of inferiority rules the mental life and can be clearly recognized in the sense of incompleteness and unfulfillment, and in the uninterrupted struggle both of individuals and humanity."
—Alfred Adler

"The most terrifying thing is to accept oneself completely."
—Carl G. Jung

Table of Contents

Foreword ix

Acknowledgments xiii

Disclaimer. xv

Orientation to Self-Acceptance 1

    Why Self-Acceptance? 1

    My Recovery from Anxiety and Depression 5

    How to Use This Workbook 10

    Life Purpose Questionnaire Pre-Test 12

    Orientation to Self-Acceptance. 14

    Nathaniel Branden's Levels of Self-Acceptance 16

    Virginia Satir's Poem on Self-Esteem. 18

Skill Area One Factors That Promote Self-Acceptance. 23

    Introduction. 23

    Feeling Good about Past Accomplishments 24

    Positive Self-Talk 27

    Coping with Setbacks and Disappointment. 30

    Self-Care. 33

    Section Summary 36

Skill Area Two Factors That Undermine Self-Acceptance 39

    Introduction. 39

    Focusing Only on Your Disabilities and
Ignoring Your Strengths, Abilities, and Potential 40

    Loss of Hope 48

    Denial of Your Mental Illness 54

    Engaging in Self-Destructive Behavior. 59

    Toxic Shame. 63

Anger 68

Section Summary 73

Skill Area Three Building Healthy Relationships 79

Introduction. 79

Establishing Relationships 80

Belonging 86

Helping Others 91

Trust 94

Coping with Rejection 98

Friendship 101

Personal Rights 106

Section Summary 110

Skill Area Four Self-Acceptance and Recovery 115

Introduction. 115

The Recovery Process 116

Beliefs Regarding Mental Illness 122

Quiz: Harmful Myths about Mental Illness 123

Schizophrenia 128

Depression. 131

Bipolar Disorder. 134

Coming to Terms with Changes in Emotions and Personality 136

Coming to Terms with Changes in Thinking 139

Coming to Terms with Family Role Changes 141

Coming to Terms with Changes in Function at Work or School. 144

Section Summary 147

Skill Area Five Developing Personal Recovery Goals 153

Life Purpose Questionnaire Post-Test 157

Vanessa's Reflections 161

End Notes. 197

Foreword

I experienced my first psychotic break in the mid-1960s. During the next few years I was hospitalized several times and, in the summer of 1968, I was picked up by the police in the street in Columbus, Ohio, and taken to a nearby state psychiatric hospital. Before long I was brought before a probate court, where I was apprised that I had schizophrenia and was being judicially committed as an insane person. I was further informed that schizophrenia is a deteriorating brain disease and that from time to time while I might appear to recover, people with schizophrenia virtually never recover. I was told that I could expect my condition to deteriorate with time, and I would probably spend the rest of my life under the care of the state psychiatric hospital system.

I later learned—thanks to the thinking of Emil Kraepelin, the German psychiatrist who more than 100 years ago first described the condition that came to be known as schizophrenia—that psychiatric professionals generally believed for most of the twentieth century that people diagnosed with schizophrenia would never recover.

Fortunately, our understanding of serious psychiatric conditions has improved greatly during the past few decades. We now have solid evidence that many, perhaps even most, people diagnosed with serious mental illness can, in fact, recover, at least to some degree. This understanding became particularly widespread with the landmark publication of *Mental Health: A Report of the Surgeon General* in 1999 and the President's New Freedom Commission on Mental Health's *Achieving the Promise: Transforming Mental Health Care in America* in 2003. The latter document's primary recommendation was to revolutionize the mental health system of the United States, with recovery as the primary goal of the new system. Subsequently, the federal government's Substance Abuse and Mental Health Administration (SAMHSA) took the lead in encouraging mental health professionals throughout the country to engage in practices oriented toward "recovery."

The term "recovery" can, of course, have different meanings to different people. Although some mental health professionals and advocates now believe that virtually anyone diagnosed with schizophrenia can totally recover, most tend to take a more measured approach to recovery. Most believe the majority of people with serious mental illness can make significant improvements with treatment but will continue to experience at least residual symptoms and remain vulnerable to episodic periods of psychosis.

This fairly recent optimism concerning the likelihood of recovery for people with serious mental illness has given rise to a variety of "recovery-oriented" approaches to caring for those of us in this population. Overall, the recovery approach emphasizes independence, autonomy, and responsibility on the part of the person with serious mental illness.

Despite these messages from national leaders, it has been difficult to overcome mental health professionals' pessimism concerning recovery for seriously mentally ill people and the tendency to marginalize them. Indeed, relatively few professionals, including psychologists, have taken a serious interest in developing and/or providing recovery-oriented services for us.

Perhaps it is not surprising that some of the first mental health professionals to forge specific recovery-oriented approaches to care received treatment for serious mental illness at one time and are now themselves "in recovery." Patricia Deegan, PhD, a psychologist who is in recovery from schizophrenia, has developed several recovery-oriented approaches. Her work on developing "shared decision making" has been particularly impressive. Beth Baxter, MD, who is also in recovery from schizophrenia, worked with Sita Diehl to develop the BRIDGES program, in which recovering people provide guidance to other people in recovery. Dan Fisher, MD, PhD, yet another psychiatrist who has been diagnosed with and hospitalized for schizophrenia, has developed a recovery approach that he calls Emotional CPR (eCPR). Information about Dr. Fisher's initiatives is available from the National Empowerment Center at http://www.power2u.org.

Of course, other mental health professionals have developed approaches to recovery-oriented care without ever experiencing serious mental illness firsthand. Examples include cognitive behavioral therapy (CBT), which uses systematic goal-oriented procedures to address dysfunctional cognitive patterns, maladaptive emotions, and self-defeating behaviors, and cognitive enhancement training (CET), which is designed to improve neurocognition, social cognition, and social adjustment for adults with schizophrenia or schizoaffective disorder.

Along these lines, it is so good to see that clinical psychologist Victor Ashear, PhD, has developed another tool for people in recovery. After working for many years with seriously mentally ill veterans under the care of the Veterans Health Administration, Dr. Ashear has drawn on his substantial experience to develop a workbook specifically to give guidance to people with serious mental illness.

With *Self-Acceptance: The Key to Recovery from Mental Illness,* Dr. Ashear has developed a step-by-step approach that focuses on improving self-acceptance to achieve optimal recovery. He delineates five skills areas on which recovering people can concentrate, providing them with a practical template which, when followed, holds the promise of adding yet another dimension to the concept of recovery-oriented care. I can see why initial feedback concerning the effectiveness of this program, which until now has primarily been employed with veterans, has been so positive.

Those of us in recovery from various forms of psychosis and other serious mental disorders greatly appreciate the skills and efforts of Dr. Ashear and other mental health professionals who are or may become similarly dedicated.

Frederick J. Frese, PhD
Associate Professor of Psychiatry
Northeast Ohio Medical University

Acknowledgments

From Victor

First, I would like to thank the late Merton Cochran, PhD, my boss at the Sheridan VA Medical Center, and the staff at the Serious Mental Illness Treatment Resource and Evaluation Center (SMITREC) at the Ann Arbor VA Center for Clinical Management Research. Dr. Cochran encouraged me to submit a proposal to SMITREC for a specialty program of intensive treatment and rehabilitation for veterans with serious mental illness, and when SMITREC accepted my proposal, he and the center's staff provided me with the resources to develop and assess the program that led to this workbook.

I want to thank my good friend and colleague Joe Graca, PhD, who worked at the Knoxville (Iowa) VA Medical Center at that time. Dr. Graca helped me refine the workbook version my staff and I initially used so we could share it with other providers. He offered considerable encouragement and support over the years and became a strong advocate for this approach.

Many staff members at the Sheridan VA Medical Center worked with me or used this workbook with their groups and provided me with feedback. I would like to mention three with whom I particularly enjoyed working: Barbara Zeigler, PhD; Karen Walmsley, LCSW; and Denise Hagney, CNA.

When I served as Recovery Coordinator for the Sheridan VA Medical Center, I worked and became familiar with Megan Harvey, PhD, Recovery Coordinator at the Denver VA Medical Center. Dr. Harvey also supported the use of this workbook and helped make it available to veterans in that facility.

Susan Blaney, MSN, FPMHNP-BC, of the Cheyenne VA Medical Center, took a special interest in the workbook and successfully used it with veterans in her care.

I have had the good fortune to work under several other supervisors who supported my use of this workbook. David Schultz, MD, nominated me for a special award based on the program on which this workbook is based. Michal Wilson, MD, and Michael Hiller, MD, were also supportive of my program and made it possible for me to continue to offer a longer-term approach when resources were slim and other programs were discontinued.

I am grateful to Dr. Robert Hutzell for granting me permission to use his Life Purpose Scale in this workbook free of charge.

Well-known psychologist and recovery movement advocate Fred Frese, PhD, showed an interest in this workbook after I gave a presentation on it at the National Alliance on Mental Illness (NAMI) Wyoming Conference in May of 2014. Dr. Frese graciously provided the excellent Foreword to this workbook.

I want to thank Vanessa Hastings, my editor and collaborator on this version of the workbook. Working with her has been a pleasure, and she finds clearer ways to say things than I do. She also has demonstrated courage in sharing the details of her experience with mental illness in this workbook, which I believe greatly enhances its value to users. I would like to thank Nancy Schenck, Executive Editor of CRP, for her gentle and able assistance in polishing this workbook into its present form.

Consultant Jack McHugh's knowledge of the publishing field has proven invaluable. Jack helped me deliver this volume to you, and I am grateful for that service.

I also want to thank my wife, Janet, who has always believed in my work and has helped me realize that this workbook is worthy of a larger audience.

Finally, I want to thank the hundreds of veterans I have had the privilege and pleasure of serving. They showed me quite clearly the power of self-acceptance to transform lives and promote recovery from mental illness. I learned as much from them as I taught them. My work with them has been the highlight of my career as a psychologist.

From Vanessa

I want to take the opportunity to thank Jackie and Ned Peterson, my aunt and uncle, for sheltering me from the storm of my early years and for always being there for me.

I also thank my husband, Adrian Chavez, and my dear friend Autum Goodspeed for sticking by my side through this difficult journey. I can't adequately express my gratitude for their dedication, compassion, and patience.

Endless thanks to Heather McIntosh, licensed professional counselor and massage therapist. She saved my life, and she constantly reminds me to appreciate the puppy dogs and rainbows of life.

Finally, I deeply appreciate Dr. Ashear for developing this workbook and for asking me to help make it available to the public. Our association and collaboration have improved my life tremendously.

Disclaimer

This workbook is in no way a substitute for medical and/or psychological treatment of mental disorders rendered by qualified healthcare professionals. As you use this book, please check with your healthcare providers to ensure the suggestions it offers are suited to your individual needs.

A Word about Evidence-Based Practice

Readers with clinical knowledge will no doubt recognize the incorporation into this workbook of some, if not all, of the evidence-based practices used to treat serious mental illness. The workbook utilizes Cognitive Behavioral Therapy (CBT), Acceptance and Commitment Therapy (ACT), and Illness Awareness and Management (IAM). In addition, as I facilitated groups over the years, I employed behavioral therapy principles, especially positive reinforcement and behavioral shaping. I would welcome a study that compares outcomes for groups using this workbook and outcomes for standard group therapy.

Orientation to Self-Acceptance

Why Self-Acceptance?

Not long ago, serious mental illnesses such as schizophrenia, bipolar disorder, and recurrent major depression, among others, often meant resignation to a life of institutionalization, a life devoid of any satisfaction or accomplishment. Fortunately, this prognosis of doom no longer applies.

With the rise of the recovery movement over the past thirty years, now more than ever before, hope exists for people diagnosed with serious mental illness to live full, meaningful lives. In fact, many people diagnosed with serious mental illness are leading normal lives that include career and family.

Improvements in the effectiveness of psychotropic medication contribute to this positive and optimistic outlook. In addition, newer forms of psychotherapy, including psychosocial rehabilitation approaches, such as social-skills training and illness awareness and management programs, have proven supportive of recovery. Most recently, cognitive enhancement therapies have been effective in improving ability to focus, organize, and problem-solve.

Even more important than these developments, in my opinion, is mental-health-services consumers' expanding awareness of the possibility of personal change and growth despite the devastating impact of mental illness. Many peer-supported and self-help resources have become available to recovering individuals. The Wellness Recovery Action Plan (WRAP),[1] developed by recovering consumer Mary Ellen Copeland, is but one example of such tools. The National Alliance on Mental Illness (NAMI) offers peer-led support groups for both consumers and family members of consumers to help recovering individuals help themselves.

With such a broad array of recovery resources, including self-help materials, what makes self-acceptance so important and why is this workbook necessary?

The Importance of Self-Acceptance

Loss of identity and self-esteem are among the most significant casualties people diagnosed with mental illness experience. For people diagnosed with schizophrenia, disorganized thinking and difficulty with accurately perceiving reality can interfere with maintaining a clear sense of self. Individuals diagnosed with bipolar disorder also struggle with identity: During the manic state of the disorder, the self may take on "grandiose" or superhuman proportions, but during the inevitable depressive state, feelings of guilt and inadequacy lead to feelings of worthlessness. For individuals diagnosed with recurring major depression or persistent depression, feelings of worthlessness may continually interfere with maintaining a realistic sense of self-esteem and a positive identity.

The nature of these illnesses can lead to a snowball effect in that diagnosed individuals commonly experience losses of employment and educational opportunity, as well as in relationships with family and friends and in other important areas of life. Because we often define ourselves by our vocational and social roles, when we lose these roles, we lose part of our identities, and this inevitably results in a diminished sense of self. This is especially true for those struggling with an already diminished sense of self due to mental illness.

In addition, stigma—negative attitudes or prejudice—associated with mental illness exerts an extremely harmful impact on consumers' identities. This stigma leads many consumers to believe they are grievously flawed, which in turn, exacerbates their illness. A 1997 online survey conducted by NAMI[2] showed that a majority of consumers were more negatively impacted by stigma than by the actual symptoms of mental illness—this even though the barriers mental illness symptoms pose to maintaining a positive sense of self are themselves substantial.

In the face of stigma and lacking a sense of self, any given diagnosed individual will feel undeserving of a life of quality, be less likely to engage in self-care, and be unable to understand that the possibility of recovery exists. Suicidal thinking may even occur. However, in spite of these devastating impacts, hope is not lost.

Patricia Deegan, PhD, is both a consumer and an advocate for diagnosed individuals, explained recovery from mental illness as a dynamic process that incorporates an individual's strengths and weaknesses. She regards it as a personal journey that includes awareness and management of the psychiatric disorder but also growing into a positive regard for oneself and meaningful life roles beyond the illness.[3] In short, the recovery process includes working toward a more positive sense of self in the face of the illness-related obstacles that threaten it.

Nathaniel Branden, PhD, defined self-acceptance in terms of being willing to take ownership and responsibility for our feelings, ideas, and behaviors without denying them and without condemning ourselves.[4] I believe self-acceptance is the most ideal way to begin the work of rebuilding and enhancing one's identity as the basis for recovery. This workbook is intended to help you as a consumer of mental health services increase your self-acceptance, enhance your sense of identity, and contribute to your growing awareness of your potential for positive change.

The Evolution of This Tool

My ideas about self-acceptance stem from a forty-year career of assisting people diagnosed with serious mental illness. I spent more than thirty-three of those years at the VA Medical Center in Sheridan, Wyoming, where I had the privilege of developing and refining programming, including this workbook, to help suffering individuals to recover. While at the VA, I had the honor of working with veterans over an extended period and the opportunity to observe the recovery process firsthand. I came to understand that even individuals with serious mental illness can recover, given supportive circumstances and appropriate tools—not the least of which is self-acceptance.

Much of the research on recovery from mental illness corroborates my experience. The next part of this introduction provides a brief overview of the history of our understanding of how mental illness and the stigma associated with mental illness undermines identity and recovery and how rebuilding one's sense of self aids recovery. Following is a sample of the distinguished theorists and psychotherapists who believed the experience of self is central to treatment of and recovery for people diagnosed with mental illness.

Paul Eugen Bleuler coined the term "schizophrenia," which literally means, "split mind."[5] Bleuler intended to convey that one of the paramount symptoms of schizophrenia is the fragmentation of the thought process, including the sense of identity. Building upon Bleuler's work, Sue Estroff, a contemporary researcher in the field of the subjective experience of people diagnosed with serious mental illness, called schizophrenia an "I am" illness, conveying that having a mental illness strongly and negatively impacts sense of identity.[6]

Alfred Adler, noted psychoanalyst and associate of Sigmund Freud, the father of psychoanalysis, was one of the earliest mental health leaders to recognize the association of mental illness and low self-esteem, which he called "the inferiority feeling."[7] Adler was also one of the first to employ psychotherapy to assist people with serious mental illness, and he regarded helping patients pursue useful roles to promote their self-esteem as a goal of treatment.

Harry S. Sullivan, also a psychoanalyst, was well known for his work in enhancing the understanding and psychotherapeutic treatment of psychotic disorders. Sullivan theorized that problems existed in what he termed the "self-system" in individuals who developed conditions such as schizophrenia.[8] Sullivan and his followers relied, in part, on improving patients' self-systems to assist them in their recovery.

Carl Rogers, renowned psychologist and originator of "client-centered therapy," worked with individuals suffering from a variety of psychological problems, including serious mental illness. He maintained that low self-esteem is a major component of all mental health problems.[9] His methods of "active listening" and "unconditional positive regard" were shown to be associated with improvement in the self-esteem of his clients and the amelioration of their symptoms.

The psychiatrist R. D. Laing devoted his career to assisting individuals diagnosed with serious mental illness. In his book, *The Divided Self,* Laing described how suffering individuals lose their connection not only to the social world but also to parts of their identities.[10]

Over the past thirty years, researchers in the field of recovery from mental illness have demonstrated several key points you might find useful in your own journey of recovery:[11]

- Mental illness contributes to confusion or impoverishment about one's sense of identity or "who I am."
- Stigma associated with mental illness also plays a huge role in eroding self-worth and identity. Stigma can exist internally, stemming from one's own negative attitudes about mental illness before illness onset, while the attitudes of other people, including family, coworkers, and neighbors, can perpetuate it.
- Recovery seems to proceed best when the diagnosed individual accepts the fact of having an illness but does not self-berate or self-stigmatize.
- Awareness of and building upon personal strengths and interests support the recovering individual. Therapeutic techniques aimed at increasing awareness about one's identity also facilitate recovery.
- Psychotherapy techniques such as cognitive behavioral therapy (CBT) can foster a more realistic and holistic sense of self, helping to improve self-acceptance and facilitate recovery.
- Peer and family relationships can be vital to promoting recovery.

The remainder of this introduction features the story of Vanessa Hastings and her experience with mental illness. Vanessa describes classic symptoms of anxiety and depression, including obsessive thinking, social withdrawal, sleep disturbances, weight gain, crying spells, fatigue, and suicidal thoughts. Depression, anxiety, and other mental illnesses are often associated with experiences of loss. In Vanessa's case, childhood losses included a separation from her parents at an early age, domestic conflict that left her with unmet needs, and a traumatizing altercation with her father during her teens.

Later, various medical problems and her father's chronic illness and early death added to her anxiety and sense of loss. Yet, she has managed to actively support her recovery from mental illness by not only relying on psychotherapy and medication but also by engaging in frank yet gentle self-reflection, moving beyond blame, allowing herself the space and time to grieve her losses, and remaining determined to rise again after each setback. I hope Vanessa's story inspires you to work toward self-acceptance and come to believe that you too can recover.

My Recovery from Anxiety and Depression

By Vanessa Hastings

As I recall my nearly lifelong battle with mental illness, I envision the phoenix, that fiery mythical creature so often depicted in slow, laborious ascent, the embers and ashes of its apparent destruction sliding from its golden wings. This imagery serves as one small component of my recovery.

The first signs of my depression surfaced in junior high, when I started to become a little edgy and cynical. Many adolescents temporarily exhibit these characteristics, but they became ingrained in my personality, protective and even fun on simmer but harmful at a boil, and my teenage angst became a long-term love/hate affair with obsessive thinking.

In high school my first serious romance thrived on and fed my dysfunction. To be fair, my boyfriend and I brought out the worst in each other, engaging in intermittent periods of verbal and physical abuse that eventually became the norm until I found the strength to break it off. My parents, divorced now for the second time, were missing in action, and I fended for myself on a number of levels. When my generally loving and doting father tried to reassert his authority during my senior year, I stood my ground; he physically attacked me, and then I moved out. These situations put me in a state of hypervigilance, a place I've visited more than a few times since then.

The transition from high school to college kicked off my first serious bout of depression. I managed to excel academically, but otherwise, I made few friends, slept often, gained weight, and cried almost constantly. My first sessions with a therapist shed some light on the roots of my distress, but I continued on a path of dysfunction, not only in my relationships with men but also in my friendships with females and in the way I conducted myself in the workplace.

Despite considerable stigma against help-seeking here in rural Wyoming, where people tend to revere stoicism, I read numerous self-help books and saw therapists through the rest of my twenties and into my early thirties, relying on one in particular to gain significant personal insight and to survive my maternal grandmother's suicide and my mother's suicide attempts. I continued to experience debilitating depressive episodes, but I sensed the key to my recovery hovering just beyond my grasp.

My epiphany came after a particularly short but destructive romantic relationship and an online study of abandonment issues. I called my dad's sister, who had taken me in during times of domestic violence between my parents throughout my childhood. "When did I first come to stay with you?" I asked.

She hesitated. "Well, you were about two and a half, and things were pretty bad between your mom and dad," she said. "I asked them if I could take you, and they agreed. We even arranged to have custody of you, so we could make decisions in case of any emergencies. In fact, I think we still have custody of you."

Despite feeling slightly stunned, I laughed a little at that. "How long did I stay with you?" I asked.

"About six months," she said, adding that I saw my parents only a few times during that period.

I felt immense pity and grief for that helpless little girl and gratitude for my aunt and uncle, who surely saved her from a much more destructive life and an early death. At the same time, I understood that any child who endures trauma, such as a lengthy separation from a primary caregiver before the age of five, is likely to suffer and struggle into adulthood.

After that call, I finally knew what was broken, and I knew I could fix it. I began to ask more questions about my past and consider its place in the bigger picture of my family's journey, partly to prevent dark history from repeating itself, partly to gain better self-understanding. But I have tried not to spend much time blaming my parents and their parents for the harsh parts of my childhood and the resulting challenges I face today. Instead, I try to compassionately view my elders as my peers in shouldering the burden of the negative aspects of our legacy. Otherwise, wallowing in blame eventually gets me stuck.

I also found that self-reflection plays a crucial role in recovery. This grueling but worthwhile process involves finding the courage and strength to study your flaws and take responsibility for them without beating yourself up, an exercise featured in this workbook. Initially, this means tuning in to, examining, and possibly changing your inner dialogue. In my case, I began to notice an anxious and critical tone to my conversations with myself. That quickly led to another crucial insight: My primary problem is anxiety, which, in turn, underlies my depression. Discussing this discovery with my therapist and friends who work in the mental health field clarified the evolution of my mental illness.

As a child growing up in a sometimes-volatile environment, I learned to prepare for the worst and remain on high alert so I could respond accordingly at the first sign of trouble. If I "failed" to ward off negative outcomes—even those beyond my control—then I took a berating not only from external sources but also myself, which exacerbated my anxiety and led to feelings of worthlessness. "Success" at keeping the peace reinforced my reliance on this survival technique, which, like any repeated behavior or activity, deeply entrenched neural pathways in my impressionable young brain, setting the stage for a general mode of operation that caused more problems than it solved in the first twenty years of my adulthood.

These discoveries and ongoing self-reflection have helped me make considerable strides over the past decade: I married a sweet and supportive man, developed healthy and mutually satisfying friendships, and improved my workplace conduct. Major life challenges during that period, however, threatened my overall recovery from mental illness.

In 2006, I moved from Casper, Wyoming, to Sheridan, a small community in the northern part of the state and my hometown, to spend time with my father and take care of him because I knew his time was short, even if he didn't. At that point, my depression was in remission, but I began to experience intense pain and spasms in my lower back, among various other symptoms. Running, which had provided me with fitness, weight-control, a competitive outlet, and a certain level of mood management, slowly became unbearably painful. A seemingly never-ending search for answers ensued, and my medical issues forced me from self-employment as a freelance writer and editor into the local nonprofit sector, where I eventually became the county's suicide prevention coordinator. As I spiraled into yet another depressive episode, I asked my gynecologist to prescribe me Cymbalta, an antidepressant my father had found useful for pain and mood management. Since half of my DNA comes from him, I reasoned, the drug would likely help me, too.

While Cymbalta somewhat alleviated my physical and emotional pain, I still could not engage in running and many of the other activities I enjoy without hurting. Believing that I deserve to live life to the fullest, I refused to give up my search for the underlying cause of my debilitation. Near the end of 2010, at the recommendation of my gynecologist, I underwent exploratory surgery, which revealed the presence of endometriosis. I opted to undergo a hysterectomy, hoping that would resolve my pain. Since I had decided early in my adulthood to forego having children for many reasons, I did not grieve the loss of my uterus. However, I chose to keep my ovaries to avoid going into surgical menopause at age thirty-seven. The procedure did help to some degree, and once I fully recovered, I was better able to narrow down another source of pain: my hip. Still, none of my local healthcare providers could pinpoint the exact nature of my problem.

At the beginning of 2012, my father became critically ill with end-stage chronic obstructive pulmonary disease (COPD) and nearly died. For several months after that episode he seemed to rally, and I fell into a false sense of security. Despite my chronic pain and because of my frustration with the side effects of Cymbalta, I decided to stop using the drug. Even with my primary care doctor's guidance, I found withdrawal physically and mentally hellish, but I eventually stabilized.

That summer, six years after the onset of my chronic pain, I saw a Denver surgeon who concluded that running on a malformed hip joint for years had caused significant damage. When he explained that he could repair the injury and that I would be able to run again, I rejoiced, and we scheduled surgery for October. That August and September, however, my father experienced his second COPD episode, ultimately receiving intensive care in Billings, Montana, 130 miles north of Sheridan. As his medical power of attorney and his only child, I spent most of that five-week period with him, watching his suffering in horror and beginning to endure the most drawn-out, excruciating heartbreak of my life.

Dad managed to pull through again, to my uneasy relief. But by the time my surgery date arrived a few weeks later, my fight or flight response was "on" twenty-four hours a day.

Completely frazzled, I agonized over the possibility that he might require another hospitalization or even die while I was in surgery or recovery six hours away in Denver. My anxiety skyrocketed as I simultaneously plunged into the deepest depression of my life.

Dad and I both made it through my surgery without incident. Managing his doctor's visits, staying on top of my physical therapy, and trying to navigate a major transition at work made my recovery particularly challenging. When I burst into tears during one of Dad's appointments, our shared physician convinced me to resume my antidepressant use; this time I chose Wellbutrin. I also began seeing my current therapist.

Around Thanksgiving, Dad endured his final hospitalization and passed away in his sleep at home just a few days after his release. Only people who have watched a loved one slowly slip away into the great unknown can understand the awful combination of devastating grief and guilt-ridden relief that follows.

As 2013 began, I made a promise to honor my father as well as myself: I would allow my grief process to unfold naturally, ignoring any societal pressure to stuff my emotions or avoid discussing my pain. At the same time, I strove to continue my recovery from surgery and to resume a normal work schedule. Six months later, my employers fired me. Undoubtedly, my job performance had declined, but the news initially came as a significant blow to my ego and my finances.

Yet, I soon began to view my firing as a blessing in disguise. I found suicide prevention gratifying, but my role had forced me to extend myself far beyond my natural boundaries as an introvert, requiring great amounts of energy without allowing enough time for rejuvenation. Now I could take time to rest, grieve my father, and resume my quiet career as a freelancer. Dr. Ashear, whom I met through the Sheridan County Suicide Prevention Coalition, asked me to help him prepare this outstanding workbook for public use; getting to know this gentle and compassionate man has been a privilege, and our collaboration sometimes feels serendipitous. I also started making a number of lifestyle changes, from incorporating vitamins and supplements into my diet to reducing my alcohol consumption to scheduling regular massages and chiropractic adjustments.

Meanwhile, just when I thought my life was beginning to settle down, I realized my hip surgery seemed less than successful overall. My physical therapist explained that my injury had left me with stretched ligaments and that no amount of strengthening would rehabilitate them completely. The implication that ongoing pelvic instability would haunt me for the rest of my life, perpetuating my chronic pain and making running impossible, crushed me.

Not long after that, I noticed the onset of new internal pain. My gynecologist suspected that my endometriosis had returned, and she advised that only the removal of my ovaries would solve the problem. So, with the first anniversary of my father's death looming among the holidays, and in the face of turning forty without his goofy rendition of "Happy Birthday to You," I chose to undergo yet another surgery. I felt uncertain about my decision for I feared I would find surgical menopause even more debilitating than living with endometriosis. Chronic pain and associated exhaustion had already overshadowed the most recent decade of my life, dulling the shine of milestones, stealing peak years of athleticism, forcing me to give up endorphin-inducing running, and ultimately worsening my depression.

After so much hardship, and with so much uncertainty ahead of me, I finally crumbled. I cried out to my father, begging him to rescue me, to pull me mercifully from the void of anesthesia into his new world, where I could rest easy with him, free of physical and emotional misery. I told my husband, my closest friends, and my therapist that I yearned for the convenience of death on the operating table, not for dramatic effect, but so that if my father did come to guide me home, they would take some measure of comfort in knowing I was ready.

As the former suicide prevention coordinator for my community, I possessed the training to recognize that I was passively suicidal, but I just didn't care. I was tired of physical pain, tired of my anxiety and depression, tired of being tired.

When I came to after my surgery, I felt both disappointed and grateful that I survived: I still longed for my father, and I dreaded continuing to live in pain, but I felt a small spark of hope that I might enjoy life again. Since then, I have continued to grieve my father on my own terms. Under the care of a naturopathic doctor in Billings, I have undergone unpleasant but successful prolotherapy treatments on my ligaments, and I have resumed running. That same doctor has helped me manage my hormone replacement therapy, and she diagnosed me with a thyroid disorder, which very likely has played a role in my depression. Treatment for that condition is proving effective, and after a long weaning process, I discontinued Wellbutrin. I take care to monitor how much responsibility I take on in all aspects of my life, and although I am not religious in the traditional sense, I have made a practice of daily prayer, which has made a positive difference.

Last but not least, going through the process of working this workbook has provided me with the opportunity to take my recovery to a new level. For one thing, sharing my story and my responses to the enclosed exercises to help you and others boosts my self-esteem. For another, the exercises have reinforced the positive strategies I previously used to cope with my struggles. I have also gained new insights, particularly understanding and acceptance of my limitations, and I am developing new coping mechanisms, most notably the ability to treat myself with the same gentleness I would extend to anyone else suffering from physical, emotional, or mental pain.

To my fellow phoenixes, this workbook will challenge you, but if you see it through, the thundering of your wing beats will soon fill your ears as you soar higher than you ever imagined. Warm wishes to you as you embark on this leg of your journey.

How to Use This Workbook

As I mentioned previously, this workbook evolved from a group workbook I developed at the Sheridan VA Medical Center. Several other VA facilities around the nation also use it in groups. As you may know, peers working together toward recovery can be quite effective. Working through this book with one or more peers would be ideal; however, if that is not feasible, you can still benefit from working through it on your own. In either case, you will likely find Vanessa's responses helpful. Her responses begin on page 161.

Your first step will be to complete the Life Purpose Questionnaire on page 12. When you have finished the workbook, you will complete the questionnaire again on page 157 to measure your recovery progress, particularly changes in your self-acceptance and sense of purpose. The rest of the workbook is divided into the following sections:

- "Orientation to Self-Acceptance" will help you gain a better understanding of the concept of self-acceptance and how you can use it to help in your recovery.
- "Skill Area One: Factors That Promote Self-Acceptance" will provide tools you can use any time you wish to work toward a more favorable view of yourself.
- "Skill Area Two: Factors That Undermine Self-Acceptance" will cover hurdles or barriers that diagnosed individuals commonly face and ways in which you might overcome any that apply to you.
- "Skill Area Three: Building Healthy Relationships" will help you explore the meaning, value, and basic elements of relationships, as well as the possibilities for improving your relationships with family, friends, and other important people in your life.
- "Skill Area Four: Self-Acceptance and Recovery" will help you explore the meaning of losses you have experienced in a new way. You will learn how accepting losses contributes to recovery.
- "Skill Area Five: Developing Personal Recovery Goals" will help you determine your readiness to make changes and identify new recovery goals.

The orientation section and each of the first four skill areas are divided into subsections. For example, Skill Area One covers:

- Feeling good about past accomplishments
- Positive self-talk
- Coping with setbacks and disappointment
- Self-care

Each subsection features a brief introduction to help you start thinking about the topic at hand. Then you will find plenty of space to respond to questions and exercises designed to help you increase your understanding of the topic and how it relates to your self-acceptance and your recovery. Writing down your answers to the questions and completing the exercises will guide you in enhancing those recovery skills you may already possess as well as develop new ones. This is especially true if you complete the exercises in order, as each of your responses will build upon the previous one. Some subsections include "homework." Completing these particular exercises will show you how to apply what you've learned to your life to enhance and enrich your recovery. Each skill area concludes with a section summary that will allow you to review what you have learned and, as a result, increase the likelihood that you will use those skills.

As you work through each section, you may wish to review Vanessa's responses as they may give you perspective on your own responses. If you become stuck on a particular question or exercise, jumping ahead to look at her work might spark your own ideas. Ultimately, there are no right or wrong answers. If you start to feel overwhelmed, remember that's normal to the hard work of recovery. Take a break, and resume your work when you're ready.

When you have completed the workbook, please keep it and periodically revisit it to refresh your memory on the skills and techniques you learned, remind yourself of the progress you have made, and encourage yourself to continue to strengthen your self-esteem and self-acceptance.

Life Purpose Questionnaire[12] Pre-Test

Mark whether you "agree" (A) or "disagree" (D) with each statement. Then use the instructions that follow to score your questionnaire.

1. I am often bored. _____

2. In general, my life seems dull. _____

3. I have definite ideas of things I want to do. _____

4. My life is meaningful. _____

5. Most days seem to be the same old thing. _____

6. If I could live my life again, I would live it pretty much the same way I have. _____

7. Retirement means a time for me to do some of the exciting things I have always wanted to do. _____

8. I have made only a little progress toward reaching my life goals. _____

9. My life is kind of empty. _____

10. If I should die today, I would feel that my life has been worthwhile. _____

11. In thinking of my life, I often wonder why I am alive. _____

12. My life does not seem to fit well into the rest of the world. _____

13. I am usually a reliable, responsible person. _____

14. People usually don't have much freedom to make their own choices. _____

15. I am not prepared for death. _____

16. Sometimes I think that suicide may be a good way out for me. _____

17. I am usually able to think of a usefulness to my life. _____

18. I have much control over my life. _____

19. My daily tasks are kind of boring. _____

20. I have discovered many reasons why I was born. _____

Give yourself one point for each of the following statements to which you answered "agree:" 3, 4, 6, 7, 10, 13, 17, 18, and 20.

Give yourself one point for each of the following statements to which you answered "disagree:" 1, 2, 5, 8, 9, 11, 12, 14, 15, 16, and 19.

Total your points for your overall score, which will range from 0 to 20.

Usually, people who feel they have few or no Meaningful and Purposeful Goals (MPGs) score from 0 to 8 points.

People who feel uncertain about whether they have MPGs usually score between 9 and 17 points.

People who have a sense of direction about some parts of their lives but remain confused about other parts also typically score between 9 and 17 points.

People who have many MPGs and a strong sense of direction about their lives often score between 18 and 20.

Orientation to Self-Acceptance

The orientation of this workbook will prepare you to use it effectively. Specifically, this section will introduce:

1. Useful terms
2. Nathaniel Branden's levels of self acceptance
3. Virginia Satir's poem on self-esteem

Purpose

The purpose of this section is to introduce you to a number of terms, the differences between them, and their impact on mental illness. With an understanding of the terms defined below, you can better develop a sense of where you stand in relation to them and how you might imagine yourself differently.

Background

Professionals, consumers, and people in general use the terms below differently. The definitions listed here are intended to make this workbook as helpful to use as possible and, in the case of group work, to ensure that shared meaning occurs during discussion.

Useful Terms

Self: Your complete physical, mental, spiritual makeup. (Who I actually am.)

Self-concept: Your idea or concept of yourself, including your ideas and feelings about your physical, mental, and spiritual aspects. Your self-concept is more limited than yourself as a whole. (Who I think I am.)

Self-acceptance: The degree to which you are comfortable with your self-concept, including your positive and negative aspects.

Self-esteem: The way in which you evaluate yourself. Your self-evaluation can be positive (feeling valuable), negative (feeling worthless), or anywhere in between.

Reflections

Why does the self include more than self-concept? What are some implications of this for you?

_____

_____

_____

_____

_____

_____

_____

Since self, self-concept, self-acceptance, and self-esteem are the result of thinking and attitudes, do you have the power to change your own thinking and attitudes? In other words, who is responsible for your self-acceptance?

_____

_____

_____

_____

_____

_____

_____

_____

Nathaniel Branden's Levels of Self-Acceptance

Purpose

The purpose of this subsection is to guide you in your examination of the concept of self-acceptance, since it is the foundation of this workbook and central to your recovery.

Background

In his book, *The Six Pillars of Self-Esteem*, Nathaniel Branden, PhD, explains how self-acceptance and self-esteem relate to each other.[13] Dr. Branden says that self-acceptance is something we "practice," and the more we practice self-acceptance, the more we can enhance our self-esteem.

Exercise

Read Dr. Branden's three levels of self-acceptance, paraphrased below, and think about how they might apply to you. Please note: You may find that considering these levels in the order in which they are presented might not be ideal for you. Feel free to study them in the order that makes the most sense to you.

First level: I am for myself. I value myself and treat myself with respect. I stand up for my right to exist. I refuse to fight with myself.

Second level: I refuse to deny my experience. I am open to looking at my actions. I don't necessarily have to admire all of my actions, but I am at least willing to own my behavior. We cannot grow without reaching this level.

Third level: I treat myself with compassion and forgive myself. I may choose to condemn some of my behavior but not *myself*.

Reflections

Do you agree with Dr. Branden that self-acceptance is a practice, something you must do actively? Why or why not?

_____

_____

_____

_____

_____

_____

_____

_____

Have you tried forgiving yourself for inappropriate or destructive behavior? Was it hard to do? What made it hard?

_____

_____

_____

_____

_____

_____

_____

_____

_____

Virginia Satir's Poem on Self-Esteem

Purpose

The purpose of this subsection is to deepen your understanding of self-esteem and how it relates to self-acceptance.

Background

Virginia Satir was a well-known therapist who believed self-esteem is essential in developing one's well-being and healthy relationships. She wrote the poem *Self-Esteem*[14] for an angry teen she wanted to help. Full of wisdom and reassurance, the poem has become widely circulated.

Exercise

Read *Self-Esteem* and think about how the poem might apply to you.

My Declaration of Self-Esteem

By Virginia Satir

I am me.

In all the world, there is no one else exactly like me.
There are persons who have some parts like me, but no one adds up exactly like me.
Therefore, everything that comes out of me is authentically mine because I alone
     choose it.

I own everything about me.
My body, including everything it does;
My mind, including all its thoughts and ideas;
My eyes, including the images of all they behold;
My feelings, whatever they may be—anger, joy, frustration, love, disappointment,
     excitement;
My mouth, and all the words that come out of it—polite, sweet or rough, correct or
     incorrect;
My voice loud or soft; and all my actions whether they be to others or to myself.

I own my fantasies, my dreams, my hopes, my fears.
I own all my triumphs and successes, all my failures and mistakes.
Because I own all of me,
I can become intimately acquainted with me.
By so doing I can love me and be friendly with me in all my parts.
I can then make it possible for all of me to work in my best interests.

I know there are aspects about myself that puzzle me, and other aspects that I do not
     know.
But as long as I am friendly and loving to myself,
I can courageously and hopefully look for the solutions to the puzzles and for ways to
     find out more about me.
However I look and sound, whatever I say and do, and whatever I think and feel at a
     given moment in time is me.

This is authentic and represents where I am at that moment in time.

When I review later how I looked and sounded, what I said and did, and how I thought and felt, some parts may turn out to be unfitting.

I can discard that which is unfitting, and keep that which proved fitting, and invent something new for that which I discarded.

I can see, hear, feel, think, say and do.

I have the tools to survive, to be close to others, to be productive, and to make sense and order out of the world of people and things outside of me.

I own me, and therefore I can engineer me. I am me and I am okay.

Reflections

What does this poem mean to you?

_____

_____

_____

_____

_____

_____

_____

_____

_____

How does Satir use this poem to demonstrate that she accepts herself?

_____

_____

_____

_____

_____

_____

_____

_____

_____

_____

What attitude does she take regarding her unknown self?

_____

_____

_____

_____

_____

_____

_____

_____

Why might she have waited until the sixth stanza before talking about changing?

_____

_____

_____

_____

_____

_____

_____

_____

Skill Area One
Factors That Promote Self-Acceptance

Introduction

Skill Area One focuses on factors that promote self-acceptance:

1. Feeling good about past accomplishments
2. Positive self-talk
3. Coping with setbacks and disappointment
4. Self-care

Each of the topics in this skill area is designed to provide you with one or more tools you can use to build your own self-acceptance.

Feeling Good about Past Accomplishments

Purpose

The purpose of this subsection is to help you understand that becoming aware of or reminding yourself of past accomplishments can inspire you to accomplish even more in the future.

Background

People recovering from mental illness often have difficulty recognizing and acknowledging their accomplishments. The way you view your accomplishments can affect your self-esteem and self-acceptance. Many people often put themselves down by comparing their accomplishments to the achievements of other people. Sometimes you may put others down by comparing their achievements to yours. In addition, you can discourage yourself by thinking, *I used to be able to accomplish this or that, but I can't now.*

Reflections

What is an accomplishment to you?

_____

_____

_____

_____

_____

_____

_____

Who decides if what you did is an accomplishment?

_____

_____

_____

_____

_____

_____

_____

_____

_____

What happens when you compare your accomplishments to those of others? Can you own your accomplishments without comparing yourself to others?

_____

_____

_____

_____

_____

_____

_____

_____

Describe one of your accomplishments. How did it make you feel?

_____

_____

_____

_____

_____

_____

_____

_____

_____

_____

_____

_____

_____

_____

Homework

Remind yourself of this accomplishment whenever you feel discouraged.

Positive Self-Talk

Purpose

This subsection will introduce you to the concept of self-talk and how it affects self-esteem and self-acceptance.

Background

Our thoughts about ourselves affect our feelings and our behavior. Such thoughts are called self-talk. People with mental illness often develop a pattern of negative thinking about themselves based on past negative experiences. When new situations arise—whether positive or negative—negative self-talk often starts automatically, chipping away at self-acceptance and discouraging them from taking positive action.

In order to counter negative self-talk, you must take three steps. First, you must identify the negative self-talk. Second, you must challenge the negative self-talk. Third, you must replace the negative self-talk with positive self-talk.

Reflections

Ask a supportive family member or friend who knows you well to help you with the last two questions.

What are some of the negative thoughts you have told yourself?

_____

_____

_____

_____

_____

_____

How can you challenge this negative thinking? Is any given negative thought completely true or only partly true?

_____

_____

_____

_____

_____

_____

_____

_____

What positive statements can you make about yourself?

_____

_____

_____

_____

_____

_____

_____

_____

_____

_____

Homework

On one side of an index card, write down one negative thought you've had about yourself, along with a challenge to that thought. On the other side, list five to ten positive qualities that you possess. Carry the card with you, and for at least thirty days in a row and at least three times a day, read the first side once and the second side ten times. Over the next month you should feel your self-acceptance grow.

Coping with Setbacks and Disappointment

Purpose

This subsection will guide you to reflect on:
- Setbacks in your life
- The disappointment you may have felt in relation to those setbacks
- How your handling of that disappointment may have affected your recovery
- How you might use various techniques to more constructively cope with setbacks and increase your self-acceptance

Background

Everyone experiences setbacks and disappointment. How you deal with these problems can diminish your self-acceptance or increase it.

One destructive way of dealing with a setback is to generalize that situation to your entire identity, viewing it as more than a one-time event and instead as proof that you are basically no good and/or a failure. For example, if you've been hospitalized for your mental illness before and a relapse results in another hospitalization, you may tell yourself that you've failed and you'll never be able to recover. In reality, relapse may be a disappointing setback, but it does not mean you failed at everything or that you will never be able to recover from your illness.

Reflections

What are some setbacks and disappointments you have experienced in the time since your mental illness began to affect your life?

_____

_____

_____

_____

_____

_____

_____

How did you deal with these setbacks and your disappointment? Which coping methods were constructive?

_____

_____

_____

_____

_____

_____

_____

_____

Did you generalize about your disappointments to include your whole self? If so, how? How can you counter that tendency?

_____

_____

_____

_____

_____

_____

_____

_____

_____

Homework

Develop a list of coping techniques for dealing with setbacks and disappointment. This can include positive self-talk and encouragement to try again. You will likely be able to develop additional ideas.

Self-Care

Purpose

The following subsection will help you explore the importance of self-care to your self-acceptance and recovery.

Background

Have you ever noticed that when you're feeling good, you tend to take care of yourself, and when you're feeling down, you tend to neglect yourself? These are natural tendencies; however, consistent self-care, even when it feels like a monumental task during rough periods, is crucial to self-acceptance and recovery from mental illness.

Reflections

What are your responsibilities in terms of taking care of yourself?

_____

_____

_____

_____

_____

_____

_____

_____

What are the connections between taking care of yourself and accepting yourself?

_____

_____

_____

_____

_____

_____

_____

_____

_____

Describe some times when you *were not* taking care of yourself. How was your self-acceptance during those times?

_____

_____

_____

_____

_____

_____

_____

_____

_____

Describe some times when you *were* taking care of yourself. How was your self-acceptance during those times?

_____

_____

_____

_____

_____

_____

_____

_____

_____

Homework

To help you take small positive steps in self-care, spend some time each day building on how well you take care of yourself. Notice if your self-acceptance improves.

Section Summary

This section focused on factors that promote self-acceptance, such as:

1. Feeling good about past accomplishments
2. Positive self-talk
3. Coping with setbacks and disappointment
4. Self-care

Summary Questions

What is your greatest accomplishment?

_____

_____

_____

_____

_____

_____

_____

_____

_____

_____

List five positive statements about yourself.

_____

_____

_____

_____

_____

_____

_____

_____

Have you generalized a disappointment into a negative thought about yourself? How did you—or could you—correct it?

_____

_____

_____

_____

_____

_____

_____

_____

_____

List five coping techniques you can use to increase your self-acceptance when you have had a setback.

_____

_____

_____

_____

_____

_____

_____

_____

What do you believe are your most important responsibilities in taking care of yourself? How does taking care of yourself support your self-acceptance?

_____

_____

_____

_____

_____

_____

_____

_____

Skill Area Two
Factors That Undermine Self-Acceptance

Introduction

Skill Area Two focuses on factors that undermine self-acceptance, such as:

1. Focusing only on your disabilities and ignoring your strengths, abilities, and potential
2. Loss of hope
3. Denial of your mental illness
4. Engaging in self-destructive behavior
5. Toxic shame
6. Anger

Focusing Only on Your Disabilities and Ignoring Your Strengths, Abilities, and Potential

Purpose

This subsection will help you discover ways in which you may have limited yourself by focusing only on your disabilities and ignoring your strengths, abilities, and potential.

Background

As an individual diagnosed with mental illness, you probably tend to define yourself in terms of your diagnosis or disability. For example, you might say, "I am a schizophrenic," rather than "I have schizophrenia." In addition, you might often fail to give yourself credit or permission for the things you can do and instead focus on the things you can't do. At times, you may even use your diagnosis or disability as a reason or an excuse for not doing something or not trying something new or difficult. In reality, you can counter these tendencies in order to achieve your full potential.

Exercise

Read "How I Perceive and Manage My Illness"[15] on the next few pages and consider how author Esso Leete achieved a goal by focusing more on ability than disability.

How I Perceive and Manage My Illness

By Esso Leete

(The following article describes some of the ongoing problems psychiatric patients encounter on a daily basis as perceived by an individual who has lived with schizophrenia for more than twenty-five years. Specific carefully planned coping strategies, which are seen as critical to the recovery process, are presented.)

More than by any other one thing, my life has been changed by schizophrenia. For the past twenty years I have lived with it and in spite of it—struggling to come to terms with it without giving in to it. Although I have fought a daily battle, it is only now that I have some sense of confidence that I will survive my ordeal. Taking responsibility for my life and developing coping mechanisms has been crucial to my recovery. I would like to share some of these with the reader now.

To maintain my mental health, I found I had to change my priorities and take better care of myself. I modified my attitudes, becoming more accepting and nonjudgmental of others. In addition, I altered my behavior and response to symptoms. I have also had to plan for the use of my time. When one has a chaotic inner existence, the structure of a predictable daily schedule makes life easier. Now, obviously structured activity can be anything, but for me it is work—a paying job, the ultimate goal. It gives me something to look forward to every day and a skill to learn and to improve. It is my motivation for getting up each morning. In addition, my hours are passed therapeutically as well as productively. As I work, I become increasingly self-confident, and my self-image is bolstered. I feel important and grownup, which replaces my usual sense of vulnerability, weakness, and incompetence. Being a member of the work force decreases stigma and contributes to acceptance by my community, which in turn makes my life easier.

Research continues to show that one of the differences between the brain of a "normal" person and one who has schizophrenia is a major difficulty filtering or screening out background noises. I am hyperalert, acutely aware of every sound or movement in my environment. I am often confused by repetitive noises or multiple stimuli and become nervous, impatient, and irritable. To deal with this, I make a deliberate effort to reduce distractions as much as possible.

I often have difficulty interacting with others socially and tend to withdraw. I have found I feel more comfortable, however, if I socialize with others who have similar interests or experiences to my own. To counteract my problem with poor eye contact, I force myself to look up from time to time, even if I have to look a little past the person with whom I am speaking. If I do become overwhelmed in a social situation, I may temporarily withdraw by going into another room (even the restroom) to be alone for a while.

I attempt to keep in touch with my feelings and to attend immediately to difficulties, including symptoms like paranoia. For example, instead of constantly worrying about the police surprising me, I always choose a seat where I can face the door, preferably with my back to a wall instead of to other people. In general, instead of working myself up emotionally over some threatening possibility, I will check out reality by asking the people I am with questions like who they are calling, where they are going, or whatever. It clears the air immediately, and usually I am satisfied with their answer and can go on about my business. In other words, I cope by recognizing and confronting my paranoid fears immediately and then moving on with my life, freeing my mind for other things. Also, I have learned to suppress paranoid responses, and I make an effort not to talk to myself or to my voices when others are nearby. It can be done through self-discipline and practice.

In addition, I suffer from feelings of isolation, alienation, and loneliness. This is difficult to deal with because on the one hand I need to be with people, but on the other hand I am frightened of it. I have come to realize my own diminished capacity for really close friendships, but also my need for many acquaintances. An ongoing and reliable support system has been extremely important. I have gained much practical information, insight, and support from my peer-run support group, a very comfortable means of coming to *accept* and *deal* with mental illness. Also, it has been invaluable to have someone I trust (often my husband) with whom I can "test reality." I let him know my perceptions and he gives me feedback. I am then able to consider the possibility that my perceptions may not be accurate, and I modify my response accordingly if I wish. In this way I can usually acknowledge more conventional ways of thinking, instead of automatically incorporating outside information into my delusional system.

A common complaint from persons with a mental illness is that of impaired concentration and memory. This can make holding a job or even completing a thought very difficult. To overcome the effects of a poor memory, I make lists and write down all information of importance. Through years of effort I have managed to develop an incredible amount of concentration, although I am only able to sustain this for relatively brief periods of time.

Sometimes I still find it difficult to keep my thoughts together. I therefore request that communication be simple, clear, and unambiguous. It helps me if the information is specific, as vague or diffuse responses only confuse me. When speaking to someone, I may need more time to think and understand before responding, and I take this time. Likewise, I have learned when working on a task to be careful, perhaps taking more time than others, and to concentrate fiercely on what I am doing. And I must be persistent.

Many times when becoming acutely ill, I am frightened of everything, feeling small and vulnerable. When I am in distress, I do whatever makes me feel better. This may be pacing, curling up into a ball, or rocking back and forth. I have found that most of these behaviors can be accomplished without appearing too strange, believe it or not. For example, I can pace by taking a walk, I can curl up when I sleep, and I can rock in a rocking chair or hammock or even by going to an amusement park. I am often able to relax by physically exercising, reading, or watching a movie. In general, then, I think I am discovering how to appear less bizarre.

I find it crucial to schedule time between events rigidly. For example, I will not agree to give two talks on the same day. I find I must also give myself as much time as I can in which to make decisions; I have an enormous amount of ambivalence, and pressure to come to a decision quickly can immobilize me. (It is not a pretty picture.) Too much free time is also detrimental. Therefore, I find it useful to structure my leisure time and to limit it. Perhaps some day I will be able to handle it in greater increments, but for now I find it best to keep very busy, with minimal amounts of leisure time.

Perhaps the coping strategy I use the most is compulsive organizing. I think a controlled environment is probably so important to me because my brain is not always manageable. Making lists organizes my thoughts. It also increases self-esteem, because when I have accomplished something and crossed it off my list, it is a very concrete indication to me that I am capable of setting a goal, working toward it, and actually accomplishing it. These "small" successes build my confidence to go out and try other things. As a part of this process, I break down tasks into small steps, taking them one at a time. Perhaps organizing and giving speeches about my illness is another coping skill—and the audience response is a type of reality testing.

In general, then, I believe I do have an irritable brain. I am super-sensitive to any stimulus. My behavior is sometimes erratic, and I am easily frustrated and extremely impulsive. I regret that I still have times of uncontrollable angry outbursts. I cope with these and other symptoms by taking low doses of medication. Before I came to realize the role medications could play in my illness, I was caught in a vicious circle. When I was off the medication, I couldn't remember how much better I had felt on it, and when I was taking the medication, I felt so good that I was convinced I did not need it. Fortunately, through many years of trial and error, I have learned what medication works best for me and when to take it to minimize side effects based on my daily schedule. Increasing my medication periodically is one means I often use for stabilization during a particularly stressful period.

I want to emphasize that stress does play a major role in my illness. There are enormous pressures that come with any new experience or new environment, and any change, positive or negative, is extremely difficult. Whatever I can do to decrease or avoid high-stress situations or environments is helpful in controlling my symptoms. In general terms, all of my coping strategies largely consist of four steps: (1) recognizing when I am feeling stressed, which is harder than it may sound; (2) identifying the stressor; (3) remembering from past experience what action helped in the same situation or a similar one; and (4) taking that action as quickly as possible. After I have identified a potential source of stress, I prepare mentally for the situation by anticipating problems. Knowing what to expect in a new situation considerably lowers my anxiety about it. In addition, I try to recognize my own particular limitations and plan in advance, setting reasonable goals.

Please understand that these are the kinds of obstacles that confront individuals with a psychiatric disorder every day. Yet we are perceived as weak. On the contrary, I believe we are among the most courageous. We struggle constantly with our raging fears and the brutality of our thoughts, and then we are subjected as well to the misunderstanding, distrust, and ongoing stigma we experience from the community. Believe me, there is nothing more devastating, discrediting, and disabling to an individual recovering from mental illness than stigma.

Life is hard with a diagnosis of schizophrenia. I can talk, but I may not be heard. I can make suggestions, but they may not be taken seriously. I can report my thoughts, but they may be seen as delusions. I can recite experiences, but they may be interpreted as fantasies. To be a patient or even ex-client is to be discounted. Your label is a reality that never leaves you; it gradually shapes an identity that is hard to shed. We must transform public attitudes and current stereotypes. Until we eliminate stigma, we will have prejudice, which will inevitably be expressed as discrimination against persons with mental illness.

We rarely read about people who have successfully dealt with their emotional problems and are making it, and they will not usually identify themselves to us because they are all too aware of the general attitude. The current image the public has of the mentally ill must be changed, not to mention that of the individual himself. We have grown up in the same society and have the same feelings about mental illness, but we must also live with the label.

Ultimately we must conquer stigma from within. As a first step—and a crucial one—it is imperative for us as clients to look within ourselves for our strengths. These strengths are the tools for rebuilding our self-image and thus our self-esteem. I found that I first had to convince myself of my worthiness, then worry about others. Each time I am successful at a task it serves to reinforce my own capabilities and boost my confidence. Just this way, persons with mental illness can and must change the views and expectations of others.

Obviously, education about mental illness is critical for all parties involved, especially for the patient. I have made an extensive study of my disorder and have found education invaluable in understanding my illness, coming to terms with it, and dealing with it. We must conscientiously and continually study our illnesses and learn for ourselves what we can do to cope with the individual disabilities we experience.

Many of us have learned to monitor symptoms to determine the status of our illness, using our coping mechanisms to prevent psychotic relapse or to seek treatment earlier, thereby reducing the number of acute episodes and hospitalizations. My own personal warning signs of decompensation include fatigue or decreased sleep; difficulty with concentration and memory; increased paranoia, delusions, and hallucinations; tenseness and irritability; agitation; and being more easily overwhelmed by my surroundings. Coping mechanisms may include withdrawing and being alone for a while; obtaining support from a friend; socializing or otherwise distracting myself from stressors; organizing my thoughts through lists; problem-solving around specific issues; or temporarily increasing my medication.

Yet, too many times our efforts to cope go unnoticed or are seen as symptoms themselves. If others understood us better, perhaps they would be more tolerant. We did not choose to be ill, but we can choose to deal with it and learn to live with it. By learning to modulate stress, we will more effectively manage our illness, thus endowing ourselves with an ongoing sense of mastery and control. I find my vulnerability to stress, anxiety, and accompanying symptoms decreases the more I am in control of my own life. Unfortunately, our progress continues to be measured by professionals with concepts like "consent" and "cooperate" and "comply" instead of "choose," insinuating that we are incapable of taking an active role as partners in our own recovery.

I see my schizophrenia as a mental disorder with a genetic predisposition, predictably expressing itself in times of extreme stress, but often exacerbated by rather ordinary fluctuations in my environment. Mental illness is a handicap with biological, psychological, and social ramifications, making it a formidable obstacle to be overcome. I understand that life may be more difficult for me than for others and that I must preside over it more attentively for this reason. As with other chronic illnesses, it has demanded that I work harder than most. I know to expect good and bad times and to make the most of the good. I take my life very seriously and do as much with it as I can when I am feeling well, because I know that I will have difficult times again and will likely lose some of my gains.

Although there is no magic answer to the [challenge] of mental illness, I contend that we need not be at its mercy. Appropriate treatment can help us understand our disease and we can learn to function in spite of it. We can overcome our illness and the myths surrounding it. We can successfully compensate for our disabilities. We can overcome the stigma, prejudice, discrimination, and rejection we have experienced and reclaim our personal validity, our dignity as individuals, and our autonomy. To do this, we must change the image of who we are and who we can become, first for ourselves and then for the public. If we do acknowledge and seriously study our illnesses; if we build on our assets; if we work to minimize our vulnerabilities by developing coping skills; if we confront our illnesses with courage and struggle with our symptoms persistently—we will successfully manage our lives and bestow our talents on society, the society that has traditionally abandoned us.

Esso Leete is Director and founder of the Denver Social Support Group and Program Director of Consumer-Centered Services of Colorado. As a primary mental health consumer, she is on many local committees and boards, as well as being the Vice President of the Client Council of the National Alliance for the Mentally Ill. She has been designated as a national Switzer Scholar and has just recently received an award for the most outstanding consumer advocate in Colorado for the last twenty-five years. She is currently employed as a Medical Records Transcriber at the Fort Logan Mental Health Center, Denver, Colorado.

Author's Note: This information about Esso Lette was written in 1989. I am not aware of her current circumstances.

Reflections

What did Esso Leete's story mean to you?

_____

_____

_____

_____

_____

_____

_____

What aspects of what she described have you experienced?

_____

_____

_____

_____

_____

_____

_____

_____

_____

In what ways did Esso focus on her abilities?

_____

_____

_____

_____

_____

_____

_____

How can focusing on your abilities lead to increased self-acceptance for you?

_____

_____

_____

_____

_____

_____

_____

Homework

Spend some time today thinking about your strengths and abilities. Make a list of them and review it often.

Loss of Hope

Purpose

This subsection will help you consider hope and hopelessness and their effect on self-acceptance in general and your self-acceptance in particular.

Background

Research and personal experience teach us that hope is necessary for recovery. Hopelessness tends to be temporary, associated with particularly low but short-lived points in life.

Reflections

What is hope to you?

_____

_____

_____

_____

_____

_____

_____

_____

_____

What is hopelessness to you?

_____

_____

_____

_____

_____

_____

_____

_____

_____

_____

What tends to happen if you lose hope?

_____

_____

_____

_____

_____

_____

_____

_____

_____

How hopeful are you about your life today?

_____

_____

_____

_____

_____

_____

_____

_____

What is causing you to feel this way?

_____

_____

_____

_____

_____

_____

_____

_____

Was there a time when you felt hopeless? If so, what was going on in your life then?

_____

_____

_____

_____

_____

_____

_____

_____

What does hopelessness do to your ability to solve problems?

_____

_____

_____

_____

_____

_____

_____

_____

_____

How does loss of hope affect your self-acceptance?

_____

_____

_____

_____

_____

_____

_____

_____

How does hopelessness affect your recovery?

_____

_____

_____

_____

_____

_____

_____

_____

_____

What allows you to regain hope? Who or what has helped you regain hope in the past?

_____

_____

_____

_____

_____

_____

_____

_____

_____

Homework

Create a list of ways to restore hope. Talk to others to learn how they have regained hope, and add their methods to your list. Refer to your list during times of hopelessness.

Denial of Your Mental Illness

Purpose

The focus of this subsection is to help you understand denial and how denial of your mental illness affects your self-acceptance.

Background

People diagnosed with mental illness often won't accept the fact of their illness until they are compelled to undergo hospitalization or other treatment, and sometimes not even then. Resistance to treatment due to denial can result in extensive setbacks to overall recovery.

Reflections

What is denial? What forms can it take in regard to mental illness? What forms, if any, has it taken for you?

_____

_____

_____

_____

_____

_____

_____

_____

Why do you sometimes ignore or deny your problems?

_____

_____

_____

_____

_____

_____

_____

_____

Where might denial lead in the long run?

_____

_____

_____

_____

_____

_____

_____

_____

What events led to your first psychiatric hospitalization or treatment?

_____

_____

_____

_____

_____

_____

_____

_____

_____

To what extent were you ignoring or denying your problems?

_____

_____

_____

_____

_____

_____

_____

_____

_____

_____

How did that work out for you?

_____

_____

_____

_____

_____

_____

_____

_____

_____

How does accepting your mental illness help you manage it better?

_____

_____

_____

_____

_____

_____

_____

_____

_____

How does managing your mental illness help your self-acceptance?

_____

_____

_____

_____

_____

_____

_____

_____

_____

_____

Homework

See if you can allow yourself to remain aware of your mental illness symptoms but avoid dwelling on them so that you can focus energy on other parts of your life.

Engaging in Self-Destructive Behavior

Purpose

In the following subsection you will learn how to address self-destructive behavior.

Background

People diagnosed with mental illness commonly engage in self-destructive behavior, which is any behavior that causes physical, mental, or emotional harm to oneself. Examples include isolating, drinking alcohol to excess or using street drugs or medication not prescribed for you while taking your prescribed medication, regularly missing work and getting fired as a result, and deliberately causing physical harm, such as cutting. Self-destructive behavior reduces self-esteem and self-acceptance. On the other hand, constructive behaviors build self-esteem and self-acceptance. These behaviors can include working toward a goal, asking for assistance, participating in a group activity, or participating in any other activity that promotes health and well-being.

Exercise

Remember a period in your life when you engaged in self-destructive behavior. Also, remember a period in your life when you engaged in constructive behavior.

Reflections

List some examples of self-destructive behavior in which you have engaged.

_____

_____

_____

_____

_____

_____

_____

_____

How was your self-acceptance when you engaged in self-destructive behavior?

_____

_____

_____

_____

_____

_____

_____

_____

_____

List some examples of constructive behavior in which you have engaged.

_____

_____

_____

_____

_____

_____

_____

_____

_____

How was your self-acceptance when you engaged in constructive behavior?

_____

_____

_____

_____

_____

_____

_____

_____

_____

Is it possible to stop self-destructive behavior when you become aware of it?

_____

_____

_____

_____

_____

_____

_____

_____

_____

Homework

Remind yourself daily of the importance of avoiding self-destructive behavior and engaging in constructive behavior in order to promote your self-acceptance and recovery.

Toxic Shame

Purpose

The purpose of this subsection is to help you examine the impact of toxic shame on self-acceptance.

Background

We will begin by studying some terms found in John Bradshaw's book, *Healing the Shame That Binds You.*[16]

Guilt: The feeling you experience when you do something you know is wrong, when you violate your personal or social standards. Often no one else is involved. You tell yourself, "I made a mistake."
Shame: The feeling you have when you violate a rule or standard in the presence of others.
Healthy shame: The temporary feeling of embarrassment that reminds you that you are less than perfect.
Toxic shame: The feeling of embarrassment when others ridicule you, put you down, call you names, or abuse you. Your natural response is to tell yourself, "I am no good. I am a mistake." A general feeling of toxic shame often results from childhood experiences with parents: Your feelings, needs, and identity become "shame-based."

Bradshaw also wrote about different ways to heal from the effects of toxic shame. The primary method he suggests is being open and willing to talk about it with a trusted person. Engaging in positive self-talk, which you learned about in Skill Area One, also helps combat toxic shame. You might think of other methods as well.

Reflections

To what degree have you experienced toxic shame?

_____

_____

_____

_____

_____

_____

_____

_____

Describe a time when you experienced toxic shame.

_____

_____

_____

_____

_____

_____

_____

_____

_____

To what extent do you blame yourself for the toxic shame you felt at that time?

_____

_____

_____

_____

_____

_____

_____

_____

How might toxic shame affect your self-acceptance?

_____

_____

_____

_____

_____

_____

_____

_____

Do you experience shame because you have mental illness?

_____

_____

_____

_____

_____

_____

_____

_____

How might talking about toxic shame with others help your self-acceptance?

_____

_____

_____

_____

_____

_____

_____

_____

_____

_____

What are some other methods of healing from toxic shame you could try?

_____

_____

_____

_____

_____

_____

_____

_____

_____

Anger

Purpose

This subsection will help you define anger, examine how anger influences self-acceptance, consider how anger can be destructive or positive, and determine negative and positive ways of handling anger.

Background

Dealing with anger can be challenging. Sometimes we express anger aggressively, hurting our loved ones in the process. Sometimes we suppress anger because we fear losing control, only to later express it through destructive behavior. Either route leads to self-loathing and decreased self-acceptance. It can be helpful to follow a three-step process in managing anger: recognize the feeling of anger, identify the cause, and then decide what to do about it.

Reflections

What is anger? Is it a feeling or an action?

_____

_____

_____

_____

_____

_____

_____

_____

Is anger always destructive?

_____

_____

_____

_____

_____

_____

_____

_____

What causes you to feel angry?

_____

_____

_____

_____

_____

_____

_____

_____

_____

How does your body react when you feel angry?

_____

_____

_____

_____

_____

_____

_____

_____

_____

_____

Why do you think managing anger is important to self-acceptance?

_____

_____

_____

_____

_____

_____

_____

_____

_____

_____

_____

Describe a recent situation in which you were angry and handled your anger poorly. Then fill in the second and third steps of the following anger-management method. As you consider your response to "Decide what to do," think about how you would have liked to handle that situation.

1. Recognize the feeling of anger

_____

_____

_____

_____

_____

_____

2. Identify the cause(s)

_____

_____

_____

_____

_____

3. Decide what to do

_____

_____

_____

_____

_____

Make a list of positive actions to take with handling anger and a list of actions to avoid.

DO:

_____

_____

_____

_____

_____

_____

_____

DON'T:

_____

_____

_____

_____

_____

_____

_____

_____

Section Summary

This section focused on factors that undermine self-acceptance:
- Focusing only on your disabilities and ignoring your strengths, abilities, and potential
- Loss of hope
- Denial of your mental illness
- Engaging in self-destructive behavior
- Toxic shame
- Anger

Summary Questions

List two personal areas of ability or potential that you have disregarded because of your mental illness.

_____

_____

_____

_____

_____

_____

_____

_____

How hopeful are you about your life today? Why?

_____

_____

_____

_____

_____

_____

_____

_____

How can you regain lost hope?

_____

_____

_____

_____

_____

_____

_____

_____

_____

_____

List two ways in which you have lived in denial of your mental illness.

_____

_____

_____

_____

_____

_____

_____

_____

Describe a self-destructive behavior and how you can stop it.

_____

_____

_____

_____

_____

_____

_____

_____

_____

_____

What is toxic shame?

_____

_____

_____

_____

_____

_____

_____

_____

_____

How can anger be positive?

_____

_____

_____

_____

_____

_____

_____

_____

_____

_____

_____

List three positive ways to cope with anger.

_____

_____

_____

_____

_____

_____

_____

_____

_____

_____

Skill Area Three
Building Healthy Relationships

Introduction

The ways you have learned to develop and engage in romantic and platonic relationships are intertwined with your self-acceptance and self-esteem. The better your self-acceptance and self-esteem, the better your relationships. The better your relationships, the better your self-acceptance and self-esteem.

Skill Area Three focuses on aspects of relationships that affect self-acceptance:

1. Establishing relationships
2. Belonging
3. Helping others
4. Trust
5. Coping with rejection
6. Friendship
7. Personal rights

Establishing Relationships

Purpose

The purpose of this subsection is to help you understand how you learned to develop relationships based on your childhood experiences and feelings.

Background

Psychiatrist Eric Berne developed the well-known form of psychotherapy called transactional analysis, which is based on the idea that improved social interaction is crucial to improving mental health. Colleague Thomas Harris, MD, wrote the best-selling book, *I'm OK—You're OK*[17] based on Berne's theories: In short, how we think and feel about ourselves influences whether we establish relationships with others and what those relationships are like. More specifically, we regard ourselves in one of two ways ("I'm OK" or "I'm not OK") and others in one of two ways ("You're OK" or "You're not OK"). In any given relationship, your viewpoint can form based on one of four possible combinations of those positions, which are outlined in the following exercise, and that combination will persist until we make a conscious choice to change.

Exercise

Read the descriptions for the following positions and answer the questions listed for each one.

1. I'm Not OK—You're OK

This is regarded as the "universal position of childhood" in which we all start the "one-down position." There, you were helpless and dependent on others to take care of you. Even though you left this period behind as you physically grew and developed, abuse, neglect, or other trauma may have prevented your thinking patterns and feelings from changing. Or you may have simply remained there.

What kinds of relationships do you think people in this position tend to develop?

_____

_____

_____

_____

_____

_____

_____

_____

Have you ever identified with this position? If so, describe your experience.

_____

_____

_____

_____

_____

_____

_____

_____

2. I'm Not OK—You're Not OK

If your parents abandoned or mistreated you during your childhood, you might believe that people are untrustworthy in general. The power of particularly negative early experiences might lead you to interpret the behavior of those who treat you well as "not OK."

What kinds of relationships do you think people in this position tend to develop?

_____

_____

_____

_____

_____

_____

_____

_____

Have you ever identified with this position? If so, describe your experience.

_____

_____

_____

_____

_____

_____

_____

_____

_____

3. I'm OK—You're Not OK

Some abused children conclude, "I'm OK by myself. It wasn't my fault; I was mistreated. It was their fault." People in this position have trouble looking inward and tend to blame others.

What kinds of relationships do you think people in this position tend to develop?

_____

_____

_____

_____

_____

_____

_____

Have you ever identified with this position? If so, describe your experience.

_____

_____

_____

_____

_____

_____

_____

4. I'm OK—You're OK

The first three positions develop subconsciously. This last position stems from a conscious, deliberate decision that can result from maturity, values, faith, and/or rational choice. Maintaining this position requires taking the time to consider various kinds of cues from others rather than impulsively acting on feelings and thinking patterns associated with negative childhood experiences.

What kinds of relationships do you think people in this position tend to develop?

_____

_____

_____

_____

_____

_____

Have you ever identified with this position? If so, describe your experience.

_____

_____

_____

_____

_____

_____

_____

_____

Reflections

Which life position fits you best or most often?

_____

_____

_____

_____

_____

_____

Based on your current life position, describe the type of relationships you usually develop.

_____

_____

_____

_____

_____

_____

_____

Homework

For the next twenty-four hours, try operating on the concept "I'm OK—You're OK." Make notes about your experience. You can decide if you want to continue operating that way afterward.

Belonging

Purpose

This subsection will help you consider what it means to feel like you belong.

Background

Everyone needs to feel that they belong to someone or something. You can feel that way by spending time with just one person or a group of people. You can also feel very alone in a group.

Reflections

What is your understanding of "belonging?" How did you learn your understanding of belonging?

_____

_____

_____

_____

_____

_____

_____

_____

_____

Describe a time in your life when you most felt a part of something, in other words, the most connected (for example, to family, a group, a spouse, or an organization).

_____

_____

_____

_____

_____

_____

_____

_____

_____

How might belonging relate to self-acceptance?

_____

_____

_____

_____

_____

_____

_____

_____

When you were first diagnosed with or treated for mental illness, what happened to your feelings of belonging? In the time since then, how have your feelings of belonging changed?

_____

_____

_____

_____

_____

_____

_____

_____

_____

Why might feelings of belonging decrease as a result of your mental illness?

_____

_____

_____

_____

_____

_____

_____

_____

_____

What is the role of belonging in establishing and maintaining relationships?

_____

_____

_____

_____

_____

_____

_____

_____

How does discovering that you have something in common with another person enhance your feelings of belonging?

_____

_____

_____

_____

_____

_____

_____

_____

How can you regain lost feelings of belonging?

_____

_____

_____

_____

_____

_____

_____

_____

_____

_____

Homework

Continue to recall positive experiences of belonging, and think about ways you might work toward feelings of belonging in your current life situation.

Helping Others

Purpose

In this subsection you will learn how helping others can improve your self-acceptance.

Background

Psychotherapist Alfred Adler, MD, developed the concept of social interest—having concern for others and the desire to help them—and he believed a strong relationship exists between social interest and self-acceptance.[18] He also believed that people who struggle with depression can feel better by helping others.

Reflections

What might be the relationship between helping others and self-acceptance? How does that work for you?

_____

_____

_____

_____

_____

_____

_____

What might be the relationship between receiving help and self-acceptance?

_____

_____

_____

_____

_____

_____

_____

Do you prefer to remain anonymous when you help others? Why or why not?

_____

_____

_____

_____

_____

_____

_____

_____

_____

_____

_____

_____

Is it easier to give or receive help? Why or why not?

_____

_____

_____

_____

_____

_____

_____

Can helping be overdone? If so, how?

_____

_____

_____

_____

_____

_____

_____

_____

Homework

For the next seven days do something to help someone each day. Pay attention to your self-acceptance during this period. Notice how helping others often improves your relationships.

Trust

Purpose

The purpose of this subsection is to help you explore the nature and importance of trust.

Background

Trust is a subject that receives a lot of attention but is not always well understood. Yet it is vital to self-acceptance and to building and maintaining healthy relationships.

Reflections

What is your definition of trust?

_____

_____

_____

_____

_____

_____

_____

_____

_____

_____

Where do you think trust begins in life?

_____

_____

_____

_____

_____

_____

_____

_____

_____

Why is trust important?

_____

_____

_____

_____

_____

_____

_____

_____

If you lack trust, how do you think you could develop it?

_____

_____

_____

_____

_____

_____

_____

_____

What might be the relationship between trust and self-acceptance?

_____

_____

_____

_____

_____

_____

_____

_____

_____

_____

What might be the relationship between trust and mental health?

_____

_____

_____

_____

_____

_____

Describe a period in your life when you trusted someone (a person or a group).

_____

_____

_____

_____

_____

_____

_____

Homework

Pay attention to the level of trust you feel with different people. Think about what influences the level of your trust in your relationships.

Coping with Rejection

Purpose

This subsection will help you consider positive ways to respond to rejection.

Background

Rejection can be extremely discouraging. However, rejection is a normal part of interacting with others. It is impossible to have relationships without experiencing rejection at least sometimes, so it is important to learn positive ways to cope in order to boost your self-acceptance.

Reflections

Describe a situation in which you felt rejected.

_____

_____

_____

_____

_____

_____

_____

_____

How did you handle or cope with that experience?

_____

_____

_____

_____

_____

_____

_____

What are some positive ways to cope with rejection? Try to identify at least three.

_____

_____

_____

_____

_____

_____

_____

_____

How might these positive ways of coping with rejection increase your self-acceptance?

_____

_____

_____

_____

_____

_____

_____

_____

_____

_____

Homework

Choose a technique for coping with rejection—perhaps even one you haven't tried before—and commit to using it in the future.

Friendship

Purpose

In this subsection you will explore the role of friendship in supporting self-esteem and self-acceptance.

Background

Many experts and laypeople agree that friendships, in addition to our connections with family, work associates, or schoolmates, play an important part in our lives.

Reflections

List four qualities you believe a true friend should have.

_____

_____

_____

_____

_____

_____

_____

_____

A true friend should:

_____

_____

_____

_____

_____

_____

_____

_____

What is the value of friendship to you?

_____

_____

_____

_____

_____

_____

_____

_____

_____

_____

What do you think makes friendship possible?

_____

_____

_____

_____

_____

_____

_____

_____

Do friendships have aspects that make them more special than other types of relationships, such as relationships with relatives or work associates? If so, describe those aspects.

_____

_____

_____

_____

_____

_____

_____

_____

How does friendship support self-acceptance?

_____

_____

_____

_____

_____

_____

_____

_____

How do you make friends?

_____

_____

_____

_____

_____

_____

_____

_____

_____

Does the number of friends you have matter to your self-acceptance?

_____

_____

_____

_____

_____

_____

_____

_____

Homework

Think about someone you'd like to get to know better and how you might do that.

Personal Rights

Purpose

The purpose of this subsection is to help you identify your personal rights and those of others and understand how respecting personal rights can lead to healthy relationships and promote self-acceptance.

Background

Your personal rights are the rights you give to yourself and extend to others. These include:
- The right to be treated with respect.
- The right to decide what you do with:
    - Your time (for example, you don't have to help a friend move if you don't want to)
    - Your body (for example, it is up to you if you want a tattoo), and
    - Your property (for example, you don't have to lend out a valued item if you don't want to).
- The right to express or withhold your feelings, needs, and preferences.

Granting these rights to yourself and others helps build and maintain more positive relationships, healthy boundaries, and self-acceptance.

Reflections

What is an example of treating another person with disrespect?

_____

_____

_____

_____

_____

_____

_____

_____

What is an example of treating yourself with disrespect?

_____

_____

_____

_____

_____

_____

_____

_____

Do you believe you deserve personal rights or that you have to earn them?

_____

_____

_____

_____

_____

_____

_____

_____

_____

Do you believe others have personal rights? Why or why not?

_____

_____

_____

_____

_____

_____

_____

_____

_____

How does honoring your own and others' personal rights lead to healthy relationships?

_____

_____

_____

_____

_____

_____

_____

How does honoring your own and others' personal rights support self-acceptance?

_____

_____

_____

_____

_____

_____

_____

Homework

Practice saying "no" respectfully, once a day, for the next week. Pay attention to how you feel when you do this.

Section Summary

This section focused on aspects of relationships that affect self-acceptance:
- Establishing relationships
- Belonging
- Helping others
- Trust
- Coping with rejection
- Friendship
- Personal rights

Summary Questions

Based on your life position, what kind of relationships do you tend to make? (Refer to pages 80–84.)

_____

_____

_____

_____

_____

_____

_____

_____

_____

In which areas of your life do you experience belonging the most?

_____

_____

_____

_____

_____

_____

_____

_____

_____

_____

What is the relationship between helping others and self-acceptance?

_____

_____

_____

_____

_____

_____

_____

_____

_____

_____

How does increased self-acceptance help you trust others more?

_____

_____

_____

_____

_____

_____

_____

_____

_____

List five positive ways to cope with rejection.

_____

_____

_____

_____

_____

_____

_____

_____

_____

_____

How can increased self-acceptance help your friendships?

_____

_____

_____

_____

_____

_____

_____

_____

_____

_____

What is the connection between personal rights and healthy relationships?

_____

_____

_____

_____

_____

_____

_____

_____

_____

_____

Skill Area Four
Self-Acceptance and Recovery

Introduction

You have gained skills that promote self-acceptance, learned about factors that undermine self-acceptance, and looked at how relationships can affect your self-acceptance. Your mental illness also can affect your self-acceptance, but at the same time, enhancing your self-acceptance can promote your recovery. Working to recover from mental illness involves accepting your symptoms and the limitations they impose. Recovery work also means coming to terms with losses. Finally, recovery involves looking beyond limitations and losses and developing and working on positive life goals.

Skill Area Four focuses on aspects of the relationship between self-acceptance and recovery:
- The recovery process
- Beliefs regarding mental illness
- Schizophrenia
- Depression
- Bipolar disorder
- Coming to terms with changes in emotions and personality
- Coming to terms with changes in thinking
- Coming to terms with family role changes
- Coming to terms with changes in function at work or school

Regardless of your diagnosis, please work the subsections on schizophrenia, depression, and bipolar disorder. You will find that mental illness symptoms overlap these disorders and having that knowledge will support your recovery in the long run.

The Recovery Process

Purpose

This subsection will introduce you to the process of recovery. You will explore how your mental illness is intertwined with your self-acceptance, learn about the role of grief work in self-acceptance and recovery, and pinpoint where you are in your own recovery.

Background

Recovery can be defined as a normal process of healing or coming to terms with loss, which is different than being cured of an ailment. In the case of mental illness, recovery is the process of rebuilding one's life in the face of related obstacles and loss, such as loss of property, loss of work, loss of relationships, and loss of functioning in a variety of areas.

It is important to note that while professionals and various tools are available to support your recovery, the hard work of the process is your responsibility. Your recovery from mental illness will depend on your self-acceptance, and your self-acceptance will depend on your efforts to remain aware of your illness and associated limitations while focusing on your strengths and potential. It is truly a delicate balancing act, but one you can manage.

In addition, having self-acceptance and using healthy coping skills will enable you to develop resilience, which is the ability to overcome adversity and loss. Coming to terms with losses resulting from your mental illness can facilitate your recovery.

The Stages of Grief

Dr. Elisabeth Kübler-Ross identified the stages of grief people commonly experience after loss.[19] Not everyone works through these stages in the same order, and some people revisit stages. Other people get stuck in the process. Here, the stages of grief are applied to living with mental illness:

- **Denial:** You refuse to admit you have a lifelong mental illness, or you minimize its effect on you.
- **Anger:** You blame someone—God, others, yourself—for your mental illness. You have passed this stage when you no longer blame.
- **Bargaining:** You make an imaginary "deal" with God, yourself, or someone else that if you behave in a particular way for a while, then you will be cured, and you will regain what you have lost.
- **Depression (despair):** You fully realize that you have a lifelong mental illness and lose hope, unable to see beyond your losses to what you still have.
- **Acceptance:** You understand that you have mental illness, but you don't blame or bargain, and you are hopeful about rebuilding your life.

We will return to the stages of grief later on in this skill area.

Reflections

What are some healthy ways to grieve losses associated with your mental illness?

_____

_____

_____

_____

_____

_____

_____

Is it necessary to set a timeline for moving through these stages? How might trying to follow a particular timeline hurt you?

_____

_____

_____

_____

_____

_____

_____

_____

How can grief work positively affect your self-acceptance?

_____

_____

_____

_____

_____

_____

_____

_____

_____

The Stages of Recovery

According to the report titled "Sense of self in recovery from severe mental illness," you can expect your recovery from mental illness to move through four stages. [20]

- **Discovering a more active self.** At this early stage of recovery, you might become aware of parts of yourself that have not been impaired by mental illness, and you might begin to imagine leading a fuller life in spite of your disorder. This stage is about imagining what might be rather than taking action.

Can you relate to this stage? If so, how?

_____

_____

_____

_____

_____

- **Taking stock of the self.** At this stage, you might begin to consider not only your limitations but also your abilities and interests, and you might develop a plan for change.

Can you relate to this stage? If so, how?

_____

_____

_____

_____

_____

_____

- **Putting the self into action.** At this stage, you might try different activities to see if they work for you. Those who experience the most success at this stage do not blame themselves when a particular activity or plan doesn't work out; they simply try something different.

Can you relate to this stage? If so, how?

_____

_____

_____

_____

_____

_____

- **Appealing to the self.** At this stage, you will have established a stronger sense of self, renewed life roles, and developed new activities. Your self will have become a refuge for coping with symptoms of mental illness and even relapses.

Can you relate to this stage? If so, how?

_____

_____

_____

_____

_____

_____

As you progress through these recovery stages, you will come to terms with your losses, and coming to terms with your losses will support your recovery.

Reflections

What stage or stages of recovery do you believe you are in?

_____

_____

_____

_____

_____

_____

Homework

Review these stages from time to time to assess your recovery progress.

Beliefs Regarding Mental Illness

Purpose

In this subsection you will examine your beliefs regarding mental illness and your potential for recovery and how you developed those beliefs.

Background

Having mental illness can profoundly affect your beliefs about yourself and your life, and your beliefs can influence your behavior. If you believe you are incapable of recovery, you will act in accordance with that belief. If you believe you are capable of recovery, you will act in accordance with that belief.

Exercise

On the next page, complete the quiz "Harmful Myths about Mental Illness," which was complied from various sources and represents a sample of commonly held beliefs.

Quiz: Harmful Myths about Mental Illness

Circle what you believe is the correct answer. Then compare your answers to those on the following pages.

1. True   False   A mental illness diagnosis is the most important aspect to know about a person.

2. True   False   The average person will not develop mental illness.

3. True   False   People with mental illness can never recover.

4. True   False   People who have been or are being treated for mental illness can't work, or, if they do, they make poor employees.

5. True   False   Positions that require responsibility and/or decision-making are generally not suitable for people who have been or are being treated for mental illness.

6. True   False   People who have been or are being treated for mental illness are generally unstable and prone to losing control.

7. True   False   Mental illness makes people violent and dangerous to society.

8. True   False   Public acceptance is greater for ex-convicts than for people who have been treated or are being treated for mental illness.

9. True   False   Mental illness is a choice.

10. True   False   People with mental illness can never be "normal."

11. True   False   If people with other handicaps can cope on their own, individuals recovering from mental illness should be able to do so, as well.

Answers: Harmful Myths about Mental Illness

1. A mental illness diagnosis is the most important aspect to know about a person.
    False: Many other aspects, such as values, talents, abilities, and interests are more important to know.

2. The average person will not develop mental illness.
    False: Mental illness can affect anyone.

3. People with mental illness can never recover.
    False: Research shows that two-thirds of people with mental illness will make significant recovery.

4. People who have been or are being treated for mental illness can't work, or, if they do, they make poor employees.
    False: Those recovering from mental illness often make excellent employees.

5. Positions that require responsibility and/or decision-making are generally not suitable for people who have been or are being treated for mental illness.
    False: Countless recovering individuals hold high-level jobs.

6. People who have been or are being treated for mental illness are generally unstable and prone to losing control.
    False: Diagnosed individuals who take appropriate medication and develop and use coping skills tend to be stable.

7. Mental illness makes people violent and dangerous to society.
    False: Research shows that diagnosed individuals are no more violent than the rest of the population. Unfortunately, they are more likely to be victims of violence.

8. Public acceptance is greater for ex-convicts than for people who have been treated or are being treated for mental illness.
    True: This is likely the result of stigma.

9. Mental illness is a choice.
   False: It is inconceivable that anyone would choose to be mentally ill.

10. People with mental illness can never be "normal."
    False: Many people with mental illness lead normal lives; they successfully work, attend school, sustain relationships, and pursue their life goals.

11. If people with other handicaps can cope on their own, individuals recovering from mental illness should be able to do so, as well.
    True: And so can you.

Reflections

What do you believe about your mental illness?

_____

_____

_____

_____

_____

_____

_____

_____

What do you believe is your potential for recovery?

_____

_____

_____

_____

_____

_____

_____

_____

_____

_____

What is the source of your beliefs about mental illness and recovery? How credible is that source?

_____

_____

_____

_____

_____

_____

_____

_____

_____

Homework

Strive to think hopeful thoughts about your recovery. Remind yourself that recovery is possible and even likely, even though it may require hard work over a long period of time.

Schizophrenia

Purpose

The purpose of this subsection is to help you recognize schizophrenia symptoms; consider how those symptoms may have affected your life; and examine how schizophrenia affects self-acceptance and therefore recovery. Bear in mind, even though you might have been given a different diagnosis you may still experience some schizophrenia symptoms.

Background

Schizophrenia is a brain disorder that tends to worsen with stressful life experiences. Schizophrenia affects thinking, feelings, and behavior and can interfere with the ability to function. Symptoms include hearing voices or other sounds that others do not hear, seeing images that others do not see, having difficulty organizing thoughts and communicating, feeling extremely suspicious and fearful of others, having unrealistic negative or overly positive thoughts about one's self, and isolating. People with schizophrenia have difficulty expressing emotion appropriately and may appear unresponsive to others. Stigma—negative attitudes or prejudice—from others makes living with schizophrenia even more difficult. "Networking," or developing ties with peers, is an effective way to deal with stigma.

Reflections

Which schizophrenia symptoms have you experienced?

_____

_____

_____

_____

_____

What problems have those symptoms caused for you?

_____

_____

_____

_____

_____

_____

_____

_____

Has stigma against the mentally ill affected you personally? How has that affected your recovery?

_____

_____

_____

_____

_____

_____

_____

_____

_____

How have stigma and the symptoms you listed affected your self-acceptance?

_____

_____

_____

_____

_____

_____

_____

_____

How can networking help your self-acceptance and recovery?

_____

_____

_____

_____

_____

_____

_____

_____

_____

Homework

Do you think your symptoms define you as a person? Putting your diagnosis aside, name some positive characteristics that help to say who you are.

Depression

Purpose

This subsection will help you recognize depression symptoms, which you can experience without actually having the disorder; consider how those symptoms may have affected your life; and examine how depression affects self-acceptance and therefore recovery.

Background

Depression is by far the most common mental illness. Approximately 9.5 percent of the US population will suffer from a depressive disorder in any given year.[21] Symptoms include feeling sad, empty, and/or hopeless; low energy; loss of motivation; loss of interest or pleasure in life activities; sleeping too much or too little; eating too much or too little; weight changes; difficulty concentrating and making decisions; feeling worthless; and thinking about suicide.

Reflections

Which symptoms of depression have you experienced?

_____

_____

_____

_____

_____

_____

_____

What problems have those symptoms caused for you?

_____

_____

_____

_____

_____

_____

_____

_____

Why do people with depression and/or other mental illnesses need support?

_____

_____

_____

_____

_____

_____

_____

_____

_____

How does depression affect self-acceptance?

_____

_____

_____

_____

_____

_____

_____

_____

_____

Homework

Do you think your symptoms define you as a person? Putting your diagnosis aside, name some positive characteristics that help to say who you are.

Bipolar Disorder

Purpose:

The purpose of this subsection is to help you recognize bipolar disorder symptoms; consider how those symptoms may have affected your life; and examine how bipolar disorder affects self-acceptance and therefore recovery. Even without a diagnosis of bipolar disorder you may have experienced some of the symptoms.

Background

The most prominent aspect of bipolar disorder is cycling between depression and mania, a state of extreme happiness or irritability. The questions in the following section will focus on mania. Specific symptoms include increased energy, racing thoughts, inflated self-esteem, decreased need for sleep, talking more than usual, jumping from topic to topic in conversation, being easily distracted, starting numerous projects but leaving them unfinished, and engaging in pleasurable but risky activity with negative consequences (e.g., promiscuity, reckless spending, speeding). These symptoms must last for at least four days in a row for a diagnosis of bipolar disorder.

Reflections

What symptoms of mania have you experienced?

_____

_____

_____

_____

_____

_____

_____

What problems have those symptoms caused for you?

_____

_____

_____

_____

_____

_____

_____

How have those problems affected your self-acceptance?

_____

_____

_____

_____

_____

_____

_____

Homework

Do you think your symptoms define you as a person? Putting your diagnosis aside, name some positive characteristics that help to say who you are.

Coming to Terms with Changes in Emotions and Personality

Purpose

The purpose of this subsection is to help you come to terms with the effects of your mental illness on your emotions and personality.

Background

Mental illness can cause profound changes in emotions and personality. Emotional changes can include loss of the ability to feel, loss of emotional control, and low or cycling mood. Personality changes can include isolating, having fewer interests, and loss of confidence. Coming to terms with these changes and associated feelings of loss can improve your self-acceptance and therefore promote your recovery.

Reflections

What was your personality like before the initial impact of your mental illness? How did it change?

_____

_____

_____

_____

_____

_____

_____

What emotional changes have taken place since the initial impact of your mental illness?

_____

_____

_____

_____

_____

_____

_____

_____

How do those changes make you feel?

_____

_____

_____

_____

_____

_____

_____

_____

_____

What stage of grief (page 117) do you believe you are in regarding those changes? Why?

_____

_____

_____

_____

_____

_____

_____

_____

_____

Homework

As you allow yourself to become more accepting of those changes, notice if your feelings change.

Coming to Terms with Changes in Thinking

Purpose

The purpose of this subsection is to help you come to terms with the effects of your mental illness on your thinking.

Background

Mental illness can cause profound changes in thinking, including difficulty with concentration, memory, and problem-solving; developing false beliefs; and having recurring disturbing thoughts, racing thoughts, and ideas that make no sense to others. Coming to terms with these changes and associated feelings of loss can improve your self-acceptance and therefore promote your recovery.

Reflections

Describe how your mental illness has affected your thinking.

_____

_____

_____

_____

_____

_____

_____

_____

How do those changes make you feel?

_____

_____

_____

_____

_____

_____

_____

What stage of grief (page 117) do you believe you are in regarding those changes? Why?

_____

_____

_____

_____

_____

_____

_____

Homework

As you allow yourself to become more accepting of those changes, notice if your feelings change.

Coming to Terms with Family Role Changes

Purpose

The purpose of this subsection is to help you come to terms with the effects of your mental illness on your roles within your family.

Background

Mental illness can cause profound changes in your roles within your family: son or daughter, sibling, parent, spouse, and others. It can also affect your sexuality. Some family members may expect you to function as you did before your mental illness began, and they may criticize you for not living up to those expectations. You might also become self-critical for not living up to your own expectations in those roles. Coming to terms with these changes and associated feelings of loss can improve your self-acceptance and therefore promote your recovery.

Reflections

How has your mental illness affected your roles within your family?

_____

_____

_____

_____

_____

_____

_____

How has your mental illness affected your sexuality?

_____

_____

_____

_____

_____

_____

_____

_____

How do those changes make you feel?

_____

_____

_____

_____

_____

_____

_____

_____

_____

_____

What stage of grief (page 117) do you believe you are in regarding those changes? Why?

_____

_____

_____

_____

_____

_____

_____

_____

_____

Homework

As you allow yourself to become more accepting of those changes, notice if your feelings change.

Coming to Terms with Changes in Function at Work or School

Purpose

The purpose of this subsection is to help you come to terms with the effects of your mental illness on your functioning at work or school.

Background

Mental illness can cause profound changes to your functioning at work or school. Some people with mental illness find they cannot participate in work or school at all. Coming to terms with these changes and associated feelings of loss can improve your self-acceptance and therefore promote your recovery, which, in turn, can increase work and education opportunities.

Reflections

Describe how your mental illness has affected your functioning at work or school.

_____

_____

_____

_____

_____

_____

_____

_____

How do those changes make you feel?

_____

_____

_____

_____

_____

_____

_____

_____

What stage of grief (page 117) do you believe you are in regarding those changes? Why?

_____

_____

_____

_____

_____

_____

_____

_____

_____

_____

Describe the work and education opportunities you see in your future.

_____

_____

_____

_____

_____

_____

_____

_____

_____

Homework

As you allow yourself to become more accepting of those changes, notice if your feelings change.

Section Summary

This section focused on aspects of the relationship between self-acceptance and recovery:

- The recovery process
- Beliefs regarding mental illness
- Schizophrenia
- Depression
- Bipolar disorder
- Coming to terms with changes in emotions and personality
- Coming to terms with changes in thinking
- Coming to terms with family role changes
- Coming to terms with changes in function at work or school

Summary Questions

What stage of recovery do you believe you are in? (Refer to your original answer on page 121.)

_____

_____

_____

_____

_____

_____

_____

_____

What do you believe is your potential for recovery? Has your current answer changed from your original answer in the section on beliefs regarding mental illness (page 126)?

_____

_____

_____

_____

_____

_____

_____

_____

In the time since the most severe period of your illness, what have you achieved in symptom reduction?

_____

_____

_____

_____

_____

_____

_____

_____

_____

What have you learned about coping skills for managing the symptoms you still experience?

_____

_____

_____

_____

_____

_____

_____

What have you learned about self-acceptance?

_____

_____

_____

_____

_____

_____

_____

_____

_____

_____

_____

Do you have a different understanding of the losses that have occurred in the time since the initial experience of your mental illness? If so, describe your understanding

_____

_____

_____

_____

_____

_____

_____

_____

Have any positive changes occurred in your life as a result of your mental illness? If so, what are they?

_____

_____

_____

_____

_____

_____

_____

_____

_____

_____

Are you starting to participate in activities you once enjoyed but gave up because of your mental illness? If so, what are they?

_____

_____

_____

_____

_____

_____

_____

_____

What new activities have you undertaken in your recovery?

_____

_____

_____

_____

_____

_____

_____

_____

What do you need to do to become more self-accepting?

_____

_____

_____

_____

_____

_____

_____

_____

_____

_____

_____

Skill Area Five
Developing Personal Recovery Goals

You have come to the last section of this workbook. Now that you've worked to heal from your losses and increase your self-acceptance, you may be ready to set new life goals. The purpose of this short section is to help you evaluate your readiness to set and work toward those goals.

Background

In order to set and achieve new life goals, especially after experiencing mental illness, you will need to:

- Have enough self-acceptance to believe in yourself
- Believe that reaching your goals is possible
- Know that you possess or can learn the skills needed to reach those goals
- Have support from people who can help you achieve your goals
- Identify the barriers you will face and develop a plan to overcome them

Reflections

Are you ready to work on a life goal? If so, what goal would you like to set?

_____

_____

_____

_____

_____

_____

_____

How does self-acceptance play a role in reaching this goal?

_____

_____

_____

_____

_____

_____

_____

_____

_____

_____

_____

What skills do you have to achieve this goal? What skills will you need?

_____

_____

_____

_____

_____

_____

_____

_____

_____

Who can support you in achieving this goal?

_____

_____

_____

_____

_____

_____

_____

_____

_____

What barriers will you face? How will you overcome them?

_____

_____

_____

_____

_____

_____

_____

_____

_____

Life Purpose Questionnaire Post-Test

When you started this workbook, you completed the Life Purpose Questionnaire. Complete the questionnaire here again, and then compare your answers and score to your original answers and score on pages 12–13 as a measure of your recovery progress, particularly changes in your self-acceptance and sense of purpose.

Mark whether you "agree" (A) or "disagree" (D) with each statement. Then use the instructions that follow to score your questionnaire.

1. I am often bored. _____

2. In general, my life seems dull. _____

3. I have definite ideas of things I want to do. _____

4. My life is meaningful. _____

5. Most days seem to be the same old thing. _____

6. If I could live my life again, I would live it pretty much the same way I have. _____

7. Retirement means a time for me to do some of the exciting things I have always wanted to do. _____

8. I have made only a little progress toward reaching my life goals. _____

9. My life is kind of empty. _____

10. If I should die today, I would feel that my life has been worthwhile. _____

11. In thinking of my life, I often wonder why I am alive. _____

12. My life does not seem to fit well into the rest of the world. _____

13. I am usually a reliable, responsible person. _____

14. People usually don't have much freedom to make their own choices. _____

15. I am not prepared for death. _____

16. Sometimes I think that suicide may be a good way out for me. _____

17. I am usually able to think of a usefulness to my life. _____

18. I have much control over my life. _____

19. My daily tasks are kind of boring. _____

20. I have discovered many reasons why I was born. _____

Give yourself one point for each of the following to which you answered "agree:" 3, 4, 6, 7, 10, 13, 17, 18, and 20.

Give yourself one point for each of the following to which you answered "disagree:" 1, 2, 5, 8, 9, 11, 12, 14, 15, 16, and 19.

Total your points for your overall score, which will range from 0 to 20.

Usually, people who feel that they have few or no Meaningful and Purposeful Goals (MPGs) score from 0 to 8 points.

People who feel uncertain about whether they have MPGs usually score between 9 and 17 points.

People who have a sense of direction about some parts of their lives but remain confused about other parts also typically score between 9 and 17 points.

People who have many MPGs and a strong sense of direction about their lives often score between 18 and 20.

Please note: Comparing the results of the Life Purpose Questionnaire Pre-test and Post-test is only one way to measure your recovery. If your score has not improved, it does not mean you have not benefitted from using this tool or have not progressed in your recovery. You can also measure your recovery by reviewing your reflections; a noticeable change in their tone and content over the course of the workbook can indicate progress. Or simply ask for feedback from your family and friends.

Congratulations on completing this workbook, and good luck with your continued recovery!

Guidelines for Group Facilitators

Thank you for facilitating group use of this self-acceptance workbook. Please go to www.centralrecoverypress.com and go to the *Self-Acceptance* book page. The information contained on this web page will support you in your efforts.

Vanessa's Reflections

This section contains Vanessa's answers to all the questions in each section. Vanessa's answers are in italics. We have included the page numbers to help you reference her answers.

Orientation to Self-Acceptance (page 1)

Life Purpose Questionnaire Pre-Test

Vanessa's Life Purpose Questionnaire Pre-Test score: 11

Orientation to Self-Acceptance

- Why does the self include more than self-concept? What are some implications of this for you?

  Since self-concept is my idea of myself, and ideas come from thinking, then self-concept is part of the mental component of myself. To me, this means that when I have a negative self-concept, remembering that I am more than my self-concept can help me expand my self-concept.

- Since self, self-concept, self-acceptance, and self-esteem are the result of thinking and attitudes, do you have the power to change your own? In other words, who is responsible for your self-acceptance?

  Yes, I have the power to change my thinking and attitudes and therefore myself, self-concept, self-acceptance, and self-esteem. This means I am responsible for my self-acceptance.

Nathaniel Branden's Levels of Self-Acceptance

- Do you agree with Dr. Branden that self-acceptance is a practice, something you must do actively? Why or why not?

  I agree that self-acceptance requires practice, especially because I have come to understand that my negative thought patterns became entrenched early in life due to trauma, especially abandonment. Abandoning those old thought patterns and establishing positive thought patterns therefore takes daily practice.

- Have you tried forgiving yourself for inappropriate or destructive behavior? Was it hard to do? What made it hard?

  Yes, I have tried to forgive myself, occasionally succeeding. For the most part, I find self-forgiveness harder than forgiving others because I tend to maintain high, sometimes unattainable standards for myself.

Virginia Satir's Poem on Self-Esteem

- What does this poem mean to you?

  This poem helped me see that while I have often succeeded in self-reflection, developing self-acceptance first would have made those efforts less painful.

- How does Satir use this poem to demonstrate that she accepts herself?

  She writes about owning her positive and negative aspects and actions and becoming friendly with the sum of those parts—in other words, herself.

- What attitude does she take regarding her unknown self?

  She is willing to take a good, hard look at herself for better self-understanding, but she understands that doing so takes both courage and self-compassion.

- Why might she have waited until the sixth stanza before talking about changing?

  The previous stanzas focus on self-acceptance, which provides a solid foundation for making the adjustments that help us become better versions of ourselves.

Skill Area One
Factors That Promote Self-Acceptance (page 23)

Feeling Good about Past Accomplishments

- What is an accomplishment to you?

  To me accomplishment means helping other people.

- Who decides if what you did is an accomplishment?

  That should be up to me, although sometimes I rely on the praise of others for validation.

- What happens when you compare your accomplishments to those of others? Can you own your accomplishments without comparing yourself to others?

  When I compare my accomplishments to those of others, I feel either haughtily superior or incredibly deficient, neither of which is productive. Sometimes I can own my accomplishments without comparing myself to others.

- Describe one of your accomplishments. How did it make you feel?

  I am fiercely proud that I followed through on my commitment to care for my father during the last year of his life.

Positive Self-Talk

- What are some of the negative thoughts you have told yourself?

  You're a downer.

  You never accomplish enough in any given day.

  You're too critical of others.

- How can you challenge this negative thinking? Is any given negative thought completely true or only partly true?

  I can challenge my negative thinking with self-talk such as:

    I am understandably a downer when I am in physical and emotional pain. I can recall plenty of times when I made others laugh or provided encouragement.

    I generally accomplish a great deal in any given day.

My critical nature, which is based in a unique ability to quickly and accurately read others, has helped me set boundaries with harmful people or avoid them altogether.

Some negative thoughts may have only some basis in reality. Meanwhile, my depression tends to make everything seem negative.

- What positive statements can you make about yourself?

  I am empathetic.

  I am a good listener.

  I can be witty.

  I am organized.

  I strike a unique balance between being analytical and being creative.

Homework

On the front of my card, I wrote:

The fact that I've been through four surgeries in three years and my father died less than a year before my last procedure is no excuse for gaining twenty pounds and struggling to lose it.

Below that, I wrote:

In spite of the nonstop major challenges of the past four years, I have remained physically active to the extent possible. As a result, I am physically strong, and these extra pounds, which I will eventually lose, accentuate my sensual curves.

On the back, I wrote:

Ten positive qualities that I possess:

I am empathetic.

I am a good listener.

I can be witty.

I am organized.

I am thoughtful.

I am strong.

I am loyal.

I am intelligent.

I am realistic.

I rarely fail to reach my goals.

Coping with Setbacks and Disappointment

- What are some setbacks and disappointments you have experienced in the time since your mental illness began to affect your life?

  The biggest setback of my life—my hip injury, surgery, recovery, and associated battle with pelvic instability—has spanned nearly a decade. This has negatively impacted every aspect of my life.

- How did you deal with these setbacks and your disappointment? Which coping methods were constructive?

  I became even more depressed as chronic pain limited and exhausted me and years passed without any hope of resolution. My negative coping methods included self-medicating with food and alcohol. My constructive coping methods included reaching out to others for support, persevering in finding the right medical care, and engaging in alternative exercise that, while less gratifying than running, supported my overall well-being.

- Did you generalize about your disappointments to include your whole self? If so, how? How can you counter that tendency?

  Yes. In this particular case, I've often thought to myself, You're prematurely falling apart. *I can counter this thought by continuing to work at my physical recovery while keeping in mind that the injury I sustained would be significant for anyone of any age but not necessarily a permanent side-liner.*

Homework

- Develop a list of coping techniques for dealing with setbacks and disappointment. This can include positive self-talk and encouragement to try again. You will likely be able to develop additional ideas.

  Positive self-talk

Taking care of myself

Envisioning myself overcoming obstacles

Journaling

Seeking perspective from my therapist and other trusted individuals

Never giving up on what matters most to me

Being gentle with myself

Self-Care

- What are your responsibilities in terms of taking care of yourself?

  Self-care—particularly eating well and getting enough rest—should be a priority for everyone, especially for those of us diagnosed with mental illness. In the end, I am the only person who I can rely on to take care of me, so I must make a practice of it to improve my life in the present and be better able to care for myself in the future. This includes carefully considering every decision I make and how it will affect my well-being.

- What are the connections between taking care of yourself and accepting yourself?

  When I take care of myself, I demonstrate that I am worthy of that care. Feeling better as a result of my self-care makes me feel proud of myself and encourages me to continue those efforts.

- Describe some times when you were not taking care of yourself. How was your self-acceptance during those times?

  Sometimes I have turned to food or alcohol for comfort, and that has negatively affected various aspects of my life, ultimately worsening my depression, which often makes me feel "less than."

- Describe some times when you were taking care of yourself. How was your self-acceptance during those times?

  Over the past year I have made numerous changes in my lifestyle, from incorporating proper nutritional supplementation to getting regular massages to buying a high-quality pillow to ensure restful and refreshing sleep. I feel these efforts have gone a long way toward strengthening my self-acceptance.

Section Summary

- What is your greatest accomplishment?

  Besides caring for my father in his final days, I spearheaded and managed the development of the Wyoming Chapter of the American Foundation for Suicide Prevention.

- List five positive statements about yourself.

  I am strong.

  I am intelligent.

  I am empathetic.

  I can be witty.

  I rarely fail to reach my goals.

- Have you generalized a disappointment into a negative thought about yourself? How did you—or could you—correct it?

  Yes. When a long but toxic friendship ended, I generalized that I am a failure when it comes to relationships. I have countered that generalization by reminding myself that in the time since the end of that friendship, I have fostered healthier and much more mutually gratifying friendships, most notably with Autum.

- List five coping techniques you can use to increase your self-acceptance when you have had a setback.

  Examining my self-care and making improvements as needed.

  Engaging in positive self-talk.

  Reaching out to trusted individuals.

  Reminding myself of past accomplishments.

  Engaging in activities that bring me joy.

- What do you believe are your most important responsibilities in taking care of yourself? How does taking care of yourself support your self-acceptance?

  My most important responsibility in taking care of myself is taking the time to consider how every decision I make will impact my well-being. Self-care leads to feeling better and, in turn, feelings of pride, which fosters self-acceptance.

Skill Area Two
Factors That Undermine Self-Acceptance (page 39)

Focusing Only on Your Disabilities and Ignoring Your Strengths,
Abilities, and Potential

- What did Esso Leete's story mean to you?

  *I identified with many of Esso's reflections on and feelings about her mental illness,
  particularly the following:*

  "I believe I do have an irritable brain. I am super-sensitive to any stimulus."

  *It took me many years to come to the same conclusion and figure out that I have more
  anxiety than the average person and that it underlies my depression.*

- What aspects of what she described have you experienced?

  I have experienced quite a bit of what she described, including the following:

  *"I attempt to keep in touch with my feelings and to attend immediately to
  difficulties . . ."*

  *For example, I know that I am especially stressed right now because I am in a period
  of intense learning at work, which comes with moments of failure, after which I feel
  incompetent, after which I feel "less than." So, having pinpointed the underlying
  cause of this stress, I realize that in order to avoid sliding into despair, I must be
  gentle with myself and counter any negative inner responses that surface. I also must
  make the effort to take breaks and engage in activities that will reduce my anxiety
  and rejuvenate my energy, such as exercise and spending time with friends.*

  *"I am hyperalert, acutely aware of every sound or movement in my environment.
  I am often confused by repetitive noises or multiple stimuli and become nervous,
  impatient, and irritable. To deal with this, I make a deliberate effort to reduce
  distractions as much as possible."*

  *For example, one of the children in my neighborhood is blowing a whistle repeatedly
  a block or two away as I write this, and I find it incredibly abrasive to my nervous
  system and disruptive to my concentration. I can't do much about that stimulus
  except tell myself it will end soon and then maybe take a break until it does.*

"Also, it has been invaluable to have someone I trust (often my husband) with whom I can 'test reality.' I let him know my perceptions and he gives me feedback. I am then able to consider the possibility that my perceptions may not be accurate, and I modify my response accordingly if I wish."

I do the same with my husband and close friends, and I find it incredibly helpful.

"Making lists organizes my thoughts. It also increases self-esteem, because when I have accomplished something and crossed it off my list, it is a very concrete indication to me that I am capable of setting a goal, working toward it, and actually accomplishing it."

I couldn't have said it better.

- In what ways did Esso focus on her abilities?

    She describes how doing her job makes her feel self-confident, important, and grown up. She also discussed the various ways in which she prevents her mental illness from taking over her life, from reducing the distractions that cause her discomfort to "faking" eye contact during certain social interactions to help her avoid becoming overwhelmed.

- How can focusing on your abilities lead to increased self-acceptance for you?

    Focusing on my abilities helps me remember that my anxiety and depression do not define me, that I can contribute to this world in spite of my mental illness, and that I have worth.

Homework

- Spend some time today thinking about your strengths and abilities. Make a list of them and review often.

    I am compassionate.

    I am intuitive.

    I am a survivor.

    I communicate well.

    I am organized.

    I am thoughtful.

    I am creative.

Loss of Hope

- What is hope to you?

  To me, hope is feeling that the future holds promise for joy.

- What is hopelessness to you?

  Hopelessness is feeling that the future holds nothing but pain and sorrow.

- What tends to happen if you lose hope?

  I tend to lose my passion for life.

- How hopeful are you about your life today?

  I am quite hopeful about my life.

- What is causing you to feel this way?

  Surviving hardship and realizing my strength makes me hopeful. Practicing gratitude for what I have makes me feel hopeful. Taking care of myself helps me feel hopeful.

- Was there a time when you felt hopeless? If so, what was going on in your life then?

  I felt extremely hopeless when my father was declining and after he died.

- What does hopelessness do to your ability to solve problems?

  Hopelessness paralyzes me physically, mentally, and emotionally.

- How does loss of hope affect your self-acceptance?

  When hopelessness paralyzes me, I feel like a failure, which makes me dislike myself.

- How does hopelessness affect your recovery?

  Hopelessness can interrupt or set back my recovery.

- What allows you to regain hope? Who or what has helped you regain hope in the past?

  I often lean on my husband, friends, and therapist when I feel hopeless. They help me gain perspective and lift my spirits. The warm sunshine, baby animals, singing birds, and budding flowers of spring also bring me hope.

Homework

- Create a list of ways to restore hope. Talk to others to learn how they have regained hope, and add their methods to your list. Refer to your list during times of hopelessness.

  Prayer

  Walking

  Yoga

  Sleeping

  Spending time with family and friends

  Spending time with pets

  Taking a hot bath

  Meditation

Denial of Your Mental Illness

- What is denial? What forms can it take in regard to mental illness? What forms, if any, has it taken for you?

  Denial is the refusal to face the truth. People facing overwhelming truth, such as a diagnosis of mental illness or other serious illness, often slip into denial. People with mental illness may engage in denial by refusing to seek help, abruptly stopping medication, or self-medicating with alcohol or other drugs. In the past, I have refused to take responsibility for managing my anxiety and depression, which was a form of denial. I've also used alcohol to reduce my anxiety rather than trying to discover and deal with its causes.

- Why do you sometimes ignore or deny your problems?

  Facing the truth is scary, and taking responsibility for my problems is hard work.

- Where might denial lead in the long run?

  In the case of mental illness, denial can worsen the condition and lead to a host of associated problems, such as loss of employment and relationships and even death.

- What events led to your first psychiatric hospitalization or treatment?

  I sought the help of a therapist when I plunged into a debilitating major depression my freshman year of college.

- To what extent were you ignoring or denying your problems?

  I knew something was terribly wrong, but I lacked the maturity and knowledge to really understand the true nature and depth of my problem. I also didn't realize how some of my own behavior was contributing to my anxiety and depression.

- How did that work out for you?

  Transferring to a different university helped me go into remission, but I continued to engage in many of the same behaviors and also endured various traumas, which led to additional periods of depression. I remained ill-equipped to deal with those dark times for many years.

- How does accepting your mental illness help you manage it better?

  Once I accepted my depression, I began to seek information about it and other mental illnesses, and I eventually realized that anxiety underlies my depression. So then I began to learn more about anxiety and how to manage it and the thinking that contributes to depression.

- How does managing your mental illness help your self-acceptance?

  Taking responsibility for and successfully managing my anxiety and depression allows me to experience joy and helps me feel empowered, capable, and deserving, which boosts my self-acceptance.

Engaging in Self-Destructive Behavior

- List some examples of self-destructive behavior in which you have engaged.

  Drinking alcohol to excess

  Overworking

  Overeating

  Isolating

  Looking for love in all the wrong places

Hanging out with false friends

Sabotaging relationships with true friends

- How was your self-acceptance when you engaged in self-destructive behavior?

  My self-acceptance was poor.

- List some examples of constructive behavior in which you have engaged.

  Reading self-help books

  Getting enough rest

  Exercising

  Eating properly

  Drinking plenty of water

  Limiting my alcohol consumption

  Taking vitamins and other supplements

  Making time for fun

  Seeking work that suits my personality type, skills, and talents

  Setting boundaries

  Developing healthy relationships

  Limiting what's on my plate

  Praying

- How was your self-acceptance when you engaged in constructive behavior?

  It's better than it's ever been.

- Is it possible to stop self-destructive behavior when you become aware of it?

  Absolutely. I think the key is looking closely at my behavior on a daily basis.

Toxic Shame

- To what degree have you experienced toxic shame?

  I have experienced intense toxic shame for extended periods throughout my life.

- Describe a time when you experienced toxic shame.

  I engaged in quite a lot of mental-illness-related destructive behavior in my late twenties and early thirties. Two "friends" separately challenged me on my destructive behavior in very unkind ways, which only deepened my inner darkness; looking back, I believe they were more concerned about my behavior's effect on them than they were about my well-being. Around the same time, Autum also held me accountable, but she did so with compassion and kindness, which helped prevent me from reacting with anger and denial. That, in turn, allowed me to begin the grueling process of self-reflection, the first stage of my recovery. During the first two years of that period, I spent a lot of time agonizing and feeling shameful over my behavior and the damage I'd caused. I also spent a lot of time punishing myself by developing and reinforcing the belief that I didn't deserve happiness because of what I had done.

- To what extent do you blame yourself for the toxic shame you felt at that time?

  I now know that taking a good hard look at myself was essential to starting my recovery, and feeling remorse over my destructive behavior was appropriate. But I also realize that dwelling on and punishing myself for that behavior only made the start to my recovery that much harder and may have even stalled my progress.

- How might toxic shame affect your self-acceptance?

  In general, we humans tend to reject "bad" people (people who commit heinous crimes, such as murder or rape). Toxic shame leads to feeling like a "bad" person. So toxic shame can lead to self-rejection.

- Do you experience shame because you have mental illness?

  I generally speak freely about my anxiety and depression to help break down stigma around mental illness and help seeking. However, sometimes I feel ashamed when I become anxious over situations or challenges that other people seem to handle with ease, and if I don't make a conscious effort to counter that shame with constructive thinking, I become depressed, my function declines, and I feel even more anxiety and shame. And so on and so forth.

- How might talking about toxic shame with others help your self-acceptance?

  When toxic shame sets in, I discuss how I'm feeling with my therapist, my close friends, and sometimes Dr. Ashear. They help me maintain perspective and remember to counter my negative thinking with constructive thinking. Sometimes others share their own feelings of toxic shame, which helps me remember I am not alone in my struggles.

- What are some other methods of healing from toxic shame you could try?

  After thinking about this question, I realized that I already use a few other methods to heal from toxic shame.

  Exercising—especially running—helps detoxify me physically, mentally, and emotionally and makes me feel strong.

  Practicing generosity—donating my time or funds to causes, supporting loved ones, treating strangers with kindness—makes me feel like a "good" person.

  Praying to my higher power on a fairly regular basis helps me do a better job of behaving with integrity, which reduces my chances of feeling toxic shame (although that's not the only reason I pray). My prayer starts with the Serenity Prayer:
  "Grant me the serenity to accept the things I cannot change, the courage to change the things I can, and the wisdom to know the difference. Help me let go of fear, shame, resentment, and rumination; act with compassion toward myself and others; make other decisions wisely; and find peace."

Anger

- What is anger? Is it a feeling or an action?

  Anger is a feeling that can drive our actions, if we let it.

- Is anger always destructive?

  Not always. Anger has provided me with fuel to achieve many goals.

- What causes you to feel angry?

  Selfishness, thoughtlessness, and cruel behavior

- How does your body react when you feel angry?

  My blood pressure rises, my muscles clench, and sometimes I get a migraine.

- Why do you think managing anger is important to self-acceptance?

  Acting on anger without thinking can cause devastating results and lead to feelings of toxic shame, which erodes self-acceptance. So making a conscious effort to manage anger can support self-acceptance.

- Describe a recent situation in which you were angry and handled your anger poorly. Then fill in the second and third steps of the following anger-management method. As you consider your response to "Decide what to do," think about how you would have liked to handle that situation.

  I was shopping at a chain grocery store one afternoon when another customer reached across the front of my cart to grab an item off the shelf without saying, "Excuse me." So I began pushing my cart forward before she stepped back. Although she didn't say anything, her body language told me she was offended, so I said, "Then get out of the (bleep)ing way" and strolled on to the next aisle.

1. **Recognize the feeling of anger**

2. **Identify the cause(s)**

    Self-entitled, rude people and the over-stimulating environment of the grocery store

3. **Decide what to do**

    Pause and remember to take the higher ground. In the future, go grocery shopping early in the morning or late in the evening, when fewer people are shopping, which will mean less stimulation.

- Make a list of positive actions to take in handling anger and a list of actions to avoid.

  DO:

  Exercise.

  Share your feelings with someone who's not involved in the situation and get his/her perspective.

  Write down your angry feelings.

  Tackle chores that allow you to be "safely violent" (beating the dust out of rugs, weeding, demolishing an old shed).

  Wait until you've calmed down before confronting the person whose behavior caused your anger.

  Pray.

  DON'T:

  Lash out physically or verbally at people or pets.

Engage in self-destructive behavior.

Drink alcohol.

Let your anger build up until you explode.

Section Summary

- List two personal areas of ability or potential that you have disregarded because your mental illness.

  I thought I could never be a leader.

  I thought I didn't deserve to find a life partner.

- How hopeful are you about your life today? Why?

  I am quite hopeful about my life because I have accepted my mental illness and I have learned how to manage it. I know that I deserve happiness.

- How can you regain lost hope?

  I can regain lost hope by praying regularly and leaning on my family, friends, and therapist.

- List two ways in which you have lived in denial of your mental illness.

  Self-medication

  Focusing on the behavior of others

- Describe a self-destructive behavior and how you can stop it.

  Choosing to hang out with disrespectful people is self-destructive. I can eliminate disrespectful people from my life and take my time in getting to know others before giving them the gift of my friendship.

- What is toxic shame?

  Toxic shame is a destructive feeling that leads to self-punishment, which prevents recovery from progressing.

- How can anger be positive?

  It is possible to channel anger to achieve goals.

- List three positive ways to cope with anger.

  I can write down my angry feelings.

  I can discuss my feelings with my therapist.

  I can go for a long, hard run.

Skill Area Three
Building Healthy Relationships (page 79)

Establishing Relationships

1. **I'm Not OK—You're OK**
   - What kinds of relationships do you think people in this position tend to develop?

     I think people in this position tend to become involved with people who will dominate or mistreat them.

   - Have you ever identified with this position? If so, describe your experience.

     Yes. In my early thirties, I briefly dated a man who liked to play head games (for example, he would disappear indefinitely and then reappear without explanation and act as though everything was fine).

2. **I'm Not OK—You're Not OK**
   - What kinds of relationships do you think people in this position tend to develop?

     I think people in this position tend to get involved in relationships in which both parties abuse each other.

   - Have you ever identified with this position? If so, describe your experience.

     Yes. My first boyfriend and I were verbally and physically abusive toward each other.

3. **I'm OK—You're Not OK**
   - What kinds of relationships do you think people in this position tend to develop?

I think people in this position tend to develop few relationships and are likely to damage or destroy the ones they do establish by engaging in abuse or other dysfunctional behavior.

- Have you ever identified with this position? If so, describe your experience.

   In my late twenties and early thirties, I engaged in a lot of destructive behavior and refused to take responsibility for my role in the sad state of my life. As a result, I lost several relationships and the trust and respect of various people.

4. **I'm OK—You're OK**
   - What kinds of relationships do you think people in this position tend to develop?

   I think people in this position tend to develop healthy, mutually beneficial relationships.

   - Have you ever identified with this position? If so, describe your experience.

   Over the past ten years, I've worked hard to become healthy and tried to use discretion in choosing friends. I now have a handful of friends I can count on and vice versa. In addition, I left behind the "bad boys" and married a kind, caring man.

Reflections

- Which life position fits you best or most often?

   These days, "I'm OK—You're OK" fits me most often.

- Based on your current life position, describe the type of relationships you usually develop.

   I like to think of myself as thoughtful, humorous, compassionate, loyal, and dependable, and I gravitate toward people with the same characteristics, assuming that we'll support each other during hard times and have fun otherwise.

Homework

- For the next twenty-four hours, try operating on the concept "I'm OK— You're OK." Make notes about your experience. You can decide if you want to continue operating that way afterward.

  I tend to feel calmer and kinder when I operate under this concept, and I find that people respond to me in the same manner.

Belonging

- What is your understanding of "belonging?" How did you learn your understanding of belonging?

  Belonging means being accepted for who I am, faults and all; being gently held accountable; and being appreciated for my gifts. I learned my understanding of belonging from my father and through therapy.

- Describe a time in your life when you most felt a part of something, in other words, the most connected (for example, to family, a group, a spouse, or an organization).

  I continue to share an extremely close bond with my father, even in the wake of his death. With the exception of our conflict when I was in high school, he always accepted me, no matter how deep my depression or how destructive my behavior. He always showed concern for my well-being and made sure I knew he loved me, especially in my darkest hours. I miss our nightly phone calls, random drives through the countryside, and occasional shared meals, but I still hear from him: One of his favorite "oldies" will play on the radio when grief over his loss overwhelms me. In addition, my mother, who has her own positive qualities, recently told me that I must have inherited the trait of selflessness from my father. I take that as the highest compliment, and it confirms that he lives on through me. We will always be connected.

- How might belonging relate to self-acceptance?

  I think belonging's relationship to self-acceptance is circular. When others accept you, you feel loveable, and it's easier to accept yourself. At the same time, if you accept yourself, others are more likely to accept you.

- When you were first diagnosed with or treated for mental illness, what happened to your feelings of belonging? In the time since then, how have your feelings of belonging changed?

  During the first semester of my first year of college, I watched my fellow freshman revel in their freedom while I sat paralyzed, completely incapable of taking pleasure in that new stage of my life. Everything and everyone seemed so foreign and eerie to me that I felt completely disconnected. Since then, my feelings of belonging have waxed and waned, generally decreasing with episodes of depression and increasing with remission. More recently, my intensive efforts to manage my illness and my selectiveness in choosing friends have drastically improved my feelings of belonging.

- Why might feelings of belonging decrease as a result of your mental illness?

  Many people lack understanding of mental illness and therefore fear and avoid those who openly struggle with it. In addition, the onset of mental illness can result in behaviors that may drive friends and family away, leading to a decrease in feelings of belonging.

- What is the role of belonging in establishing and maintaining relationships?

  Belonging is the foundation of establishing and maintaining healthy relationships.

- How does discovering that you have something in common with another person enhance your feelings of belonging?

  Shared life experiences and interests support the formation of bonds and, in turn, feelings of belonging.

- How can you regain lost feelings of belonging?

  Trying to repair relationships that I damaged or develop new relationships can help restore lost feelings of belonging. I think continuing to seek out the company of those who understand mental illness—either firsthand or from an outside perspective—would be especially helpful.

Helping Others

- What might be the relationship between helping others and self-acceptance? How does that work for you?

Helping others gives me the greatest sense of having value as a person, and when I experience that feeling, accepting myself is much easier.

- What might be the relationship between receiving help and self-acceptance?

  When others take the time to help me when I'm struggling, I know they value me. Then I think, If other people value me, then they accept me, so I should value and accept myself, too.

- Do you prefer to remain anonymous when you help others? Why or why not?

  Usually when I help others, circumstances prevent anonymity. For example, when I hear that a friend is struggling, I will call him/her to ask what I can do to help. While feeling appreciated for helping certainly is nice, helping anonymously and without the expectation of acknowledgment probably would be more altruistic.

- Is it easier to give or receive help? Why or why not?

  When others help me, I sometimes feel like I'm draining them, so giving help is easier for me.

- Can helping be overdone? If so, how?

  Yes. Some people spend so much time helping others that they forget to take care of themselves.

Trust

- What is your definition of trust?

  Trust is a feeling that develops between two people when they prove that they can rely on each other in good times and bad times and share experiences, thoughts, and feelings with each other without fear of ridicule, rejection, or breach of confidentiality.

- Where do you think trust begins in life?

  Trust begins to form immediately after birth.

- Why is trust important?

  Healthy relationships are founded on trust.

- If you lack trust, how do you think you could develop it?

  Sometimes I trust people too quickly, and then I get burned. I think it's important to take the time to really get to know people before trusting them. It's also important to tune in to and trust my intuition about people, especially when everything seems fine on the surface.

- What might be the relationship between trust and self-acceptance?

  If you can trust yourself, it's easier to accept yourself. Also, when you trust others, and they prove that trust is valid, then it is easier to trust your judgment and therefore accept yourself.

- What might be the relationship between trust and mental health?

  If you trust yourself, then you know you have the power to do everything you can—including surrounding yourself with people you know you can trust—to support your mental health.

- Describe a period in your life when you trusted someone (a person or a group).

  One day early in my journey through chronic pain, my future husband and I were lying on the bed we shared, talking about life in general. I felt particularly depressed at that time and expressed my fear that he would eventually find my physical and mental health issues burdensome and then leave me. He spontaneously slid off the bed, got down on one knee, took my hand, and asked me to marry him. Since then, he has stood by my side as I struggled to survive the hardest experiences of my life. He has endured the peaks of my anxiety and the valleys of my depression. As a result, I trust that his support will continue, and I strive to support him.

Coping with Rejection

- Describe a situation in which you felt rejected.

  After a long-term romantic relationship ended in my late twenties, I was very needy and therefore took little care in choosing the men I dated. As a result, those relationships didn't last very long. However, I felt devastatingly rejected in each case, even when I was the rejecter.

- How did you handle or cope with the experience?

  I partied—a lot—which made me feel worse in the long run.

- What are some positive ways to cope with rejection? Try to identify at least three.

  Journaling

  Exercising

  Talking with a trusted friend or mental health professional

  Avoiding alcohol

- How might these positive ways of coping with rejection increase your self-acceptance?

  When you treat yourself gently and with respect rather than engaging in self-destructive behaviors in the wake of rejection, self-acceptance is easier.

Friendship

- List four qualities that you believe a true friend should have.

  A true friend should:

  Be reliable

  Be empathetic

  Be honest

  Have a sense of humor

- What is the value of friendship to you?

  Friendship is essential to my life. I would suffer without it.

- What do you think makes friendship possible?

  In any given friendship, both parties must be willing to continually nurture the relationship. That means making an effort to stay in touch, spend time together, and support each other during difficult times.

- Do friendships have aspects that make them more special than other types of relationships, such as relationships with family or work associates? If so, describe those aspects.

You generally know that friends truly want your companionship, whereas family and work associates are more likely to feel obligated to spend time with you. I also think true friends are more likely than family or work associates to accept you for who you really are.

- How does friendship support self-acceptance?

  The fact that my friends aren't obligated to spend time with me but still want my company anyway makes me feel special, and that makes self-acceptance easier.

- How do you make friends?

  After I first meet a person, I generally pick up on various cues that let me know whether we're on the same wavelength. If it seems that we are, then I will seek one-on-one time with that person, perhaps through a coffee or lunch date. Our conversation during that get-together will let me know if the potential for a lasting bond exists. If so, then I'll continue to make efforts to call and hang out, as long as the other person does, too. In some cases, people seek out my friendship, and things unfold in much the same way.

- Does the number of friends you have matter to your self-acceptance?

  No. I prefer quality to quantity.

Personal Rights

- What is an example of treating another person with disrespect?

  Interrupting during conversation is an example of treating others with disrespect.

- What is an example of treating yourself with disrespect?

  Working without taking a break is an example of self-disrespect.

- Do you believe you deserve personal rights or that you have to earn them?

  Looking back, it seems like I've spent most of my life feeling like I had to earn personal rights. Only recently have I come to believe that I deserve personal rights.

- Do you believe others have personal rights? Why or why not?

I believe all of us are born with the right to be treated with respect and the right to express or withhold our feelings, needs, and preferences. At the same time, children, lacking maturity, fully developed motor skills, and the ability to consistently make wise decisions, should not have free reign to decide what to do with their time, bodies, or property. And individuals who have been imprisoned for heinous crimes such as murder or rape deserve to lose their personal rights.

- How does honoring your own and others' personal rights lead to healthy relationships?

  Doing so fosters feelings of mutual respect and respectful behavior.

- How does honoring your own and others' personal rights support self-acceptance?

  Doing so creates the feeling that everyone is equal and that we're all in this together, and that makes self-acceptance easier.

Section Summary

- Based on your position in life, what kind of relationships do you tend to make?

  "I'm OK – You're OK"

- In which areas of your life do you experience belonging the most?

  In my marriage and my friendships.

- What is the relationship between helping others and self-acceptance?

  Helping others gives me the greatest sense of having value as a person, which makes it easier to accept myself.

- How does increased self-acceptance help you trust others more?

  My self-acceptance leads me to feel confident in my ability to accurately determine who is trustworthy and who is not and then proceed accordingly.

- List five positive ways to cope with rejection.

  Spending time with family or friends

  Spending time outdoors

Journaling

Praying

Talking about it with a therapist

- How can increased self-acceptance help your friendships?

  Increased self-acceptance helps me recognize and appreciate true friends and let go of the rest.

- What is the connection between personal rights and healthy relationships?

  Mutual respect for personal rights leads to healthy relationships.

Skill Area Four
Self-Acceptance and Recovery (page 115)

The Recovery Process

- What are some healthy ways to grieve losses associated with your mental illness?

  Journaling

  Praying

  Talking with a therapist

  Reviewing the stages of grief to remember that the process is normal

- Is it necessary to set a timeline for moving through these stages? How might trying to follow a particular timeline hurt you?

  I think it's harmful to set a timeline for grief associated with any loss. The process, which is unique to each person, is already difficult enough to survive without that added pressure.

- How can grief work positively affect your self-acceptance?

  Grief work allows you to come to terms with your losses, clearing the way to focus on what you still have.

According to the report titled "Sense of self in recovery from severe mental illness," you can expect your recovery from mental illness to move through four stages:

Discovering a more active self

- Can you relate to this stage? If so, how?

  Yes. I recall feeling compassion for others even as a child. I think my compassion has grown over the years, not only in spite of my depression, but also because of it.

Taking stock of the self

- Can you relate to this stage? If so, how?

  Yes. Once I educated myself about mental illness, I felt relieved to realize that, like any other disease (diabetes, arthritis), generalized anxiety and depression come with limitations. That seemed to reduce the agony I've felt over my inability to function "normally," and I gave myself permission to figure out what's normal for me and make changes to support that. This included reassessing my career goals: I decided to return to what comes naturally to me (writing and editing), to seek employment that allowed me to work from home, and to consider working fewer than forty hours a week.

Putting the self into action

- Can you relate to this stage? If so, how?

  Yes. After years of submitting traditional applications for telecommute editorial jobs, I decided to ditch my standard resume, create a unique promotional packet, and send out two copies of it each week. Within six months, I caught the attention of my current employer, a national environmental consulting firm with local offices, and I now serve as a technical writer/editor/marketing assistant and work from home.

Appealing to the self

- Can you relate to this stage? If so, how?

  Yes. When my stress level feels manageable, I feel comfortable in my own skin and confident in my roles as wife, friend, mental-health advocate, and writer/editor. I am more willing to try new activities. Even when my confidence begins to erode and

I start to slide back into depression, I am able to recognize what's happening and why, take deliberate steps to improve my stress management, and then soothe myself, to some degree.

Reflections

- What stage or stages of recovery do you believe you are in?

  I think I'm moving back and forth between the "putting the self into action" and "appealing to the self" stages.

Beliefs Regarding Mental Illness

- What do you believe about your mental illness?

  Sometimes I believe it is a curse. Sometimes I believe my life's purpose is to use my experience to help others with mental illness.

- What do you believe is your potential for recovery?

  As time passes, I become more certain that I can make significant progress with my recovery.

- What is the source of your beliefs about mental illness and recovery? How credible is that source?

  I am the source of my beliefs about mental illness and recovery. I am credible as long as I am willing to consider various perspectives in forming and altering my beliefs.

Schizophrenia

- Which schizophrenia symptoms have you experienced?

  Having difficulty organizing thoughts

  Feeling suspicious and fearful of others

  Having unrealistic negative thoughts about myself

  Isolating

- What problems have those symptoms caused for you?

  Those symptoms have caused problems in my personal relationships and the workplace. They also have led to feelings of worthlessness.

- Has stigma against the mentally ill affected you personally? How has that affected your recovery?

  I have found others' comments about mental illness offensive, but I don't recall anyone saying anything offensive about my depression in particular. However, I believe that some people in my life have lacked understanding of mental illness and have not known how to appropriately respond to me when my symptoms were obvious or worsening. They just thought I was being difficult and responded with anger, impatience, condescension, and/or distancing, which generally worsened my depression.

- How have stigma and the symptoms you listed affected your self-acceptance?

  The symptoms I listed have often led me to wonder, "What's wrong with me? Why can't I be 'normal,' like everyone else?" I suppose that's self-stigmatization. It definitely makes self-acceptance difficult. Years ago, stigma from others may have compounded my mental illness and made self-acceptance difficult; however, since then, accepting my anxiety and depression has allowed me to speak out about mental illness in general in an effort to reduce stigma, and that has supported my self-acceptance.

- How can networking help your self-acceptance and recovery?

  Knowing that others share similar experiences and associated feelings due to mental illness goes a long way toward self-acceptance, and, in turn, recovery.

Depression

- Which symptoms of depression have you experienced?

  I have experienced all of them.

- What problems have those symptoms caused for you?

  Those symptoms have affected my self-esteem, my desire and ability to function, and my personal and professional relationships. I've never developed a plan for killing myself, but at times I've welcomed death as an escape from the pain of those symptoms, and that's passive suicidal ideation.

- Why do people with depression and/or other mental illnesses need support?

  Support helps people with mental illness manage their condition so they can live long, satisfying, and productive lives.

- How does depression affect self-acceptance?

  Without management, depression chips away at self-acceptance like a relentless jackhammer.

Bipolar Disorder

- What symptoms of mania have you experienced?

  Years ago, I engaged in pleasurable but risky activity with negative consequences, such as dating "bad boys," reckless spending, and careless driving.

  Sometimes, my anxiety causes racing thoughts.

- What problems have those symptoms caused for you?

  Dating "bad boys" caused me heartache and reduced my self-esteem. Reckless spending and careless driving resulted in financial difficulties, frustration, and reduced self-esteem.

  When I have racing thoughts, I have trouble sleeping, and that makes functioning more difficult, which causes me more anxiety.

- How have those problems affected your self-acceptance?

  They have made self-acceptance difficult.

Coming to Terms with Changes in Emotions and Personality

- What was your personality like before the initial impact of your mental illness? How did it change?

  I remember being much more lighthearted and carefree. Nowadays, people tend to describe me as "intense."

- What emotional changes have taken place since the initial impact of your mental illness?

  Anger has played a central role in my life since then. Due to a lot of hard work on my part, however, it's not as pervasive as it used to be.

- How do those changes make you feel?

  Sometimes I feel resentful, but for the most part, I have come to revel in my intensity, and I have learned to control my anger and make effective use of it when necessary. And to those who cannot accept those aspects of me, I say, "If you can't take the heat, then get out of the kitchen."

- What stage of grief do you believe you are in regarding those changes? Why?

  I believe I am in the acceptance stage of grief regarding those changes, because I have examined them, addressed them as I see fit, and carried on.

Coming to Terms with Changes in Thinking

- Describe how your mental illness has affected your thinking.

  Anxiety causes me to have racing thoughts, which lead to trouble with concentration and problem-solving. Depression, on the other hand, causes me to have sluggish thinking, which also leads to trouble with concentration and problem solving.

- How do those changes make you feel?

  I often feel frustrated, defective, and fearful that those impairments will lead to loss of employment and loss of relationships.

- What stage of grief do you believe you are in regarding those changes? Why?

  I believe I am in the despair stage of grief regarding those changes, because I often can't see all that I have achieved and all of the love and respect I have received in spite of them.

Coming to Terms with Family Role Changes

- How has your mental illness affected your roles within your family?

  Sometimes I feel like a failure as a wife, especially when I am just trying to get through the day and lack the desire and energy to deal with meals, cleaning, taking care of our pets, etc. During my darkest periods, I tend to feel that I am a physical and emotional burden to my husband.

- How has your mental illness affected your sexuality?

  I put on twenty pounds during the past few years and now struggle daily to lose that weight. I recognize that my grief over losing my father, multiple surgeries, entry into surgical menopause, and past use of antidepressants accounts for that weight gain, to a degree. I also suspect that my anxiety and depression work against my intensive efforts to lose that weight. Regardless, I feel far less attractive than I used to feel, and that, along with the loss of my ovaries, has significantly reduced my sex drive.

- How do those changes make you feel?

  Those changes make me feel extremely sad, resentful, and hopeless.

- What stage of grief do you believe you are in regarding those changes? Why?

  I think I tend to cycle between denial, anger, bargaining, and despair in regard to the effects of my mental illness on my marriage and my sexuality, because I can't even consider accepting them. I still believe I can recover from my hardships, anxiety, and depression and regain my vitality and sexuality.

Coming to Terms with Changes in Function at Work or School

- Describe how your mental illness has affected your functioning at work or school.

  Sometimes my mental illness affects my concentration and drive. It also has strained my relationships with coworkers. In some cases, I felt frustrated and resentful that my coworkers didn't understand or were insensitive to my anxiety and depression. In other cases, the irritability and negativity that accompanies my mental illness made it difficult for me to get along with coworkers.

- How do those changes make you feel?

  When depression saps my drive and my ability to concentrate, I become anxious about my productivity, and that, in turn, makes me feel more depressed. I can't do much to change my past difficulties with co-workers, but today I work hard to manage my symptoms when I'm interacting with others in the workplace, and I feel pretty satisfied with my efforts.

- What stage of grief do you believe you are in regarding those changes? Why?

  I think I have accepted these changes, as evidenced by my recent decision to secure a work-at-home arrangement. I realized that working at home fuels my energy, makes it easier for me to concentrate, and reduces the chances that I will negatively interact with my coworkers.

- Describe the work and education opportunities you see in your future.

  I plan on continuing to work at home for my current firm, which encourages and supports continuing education, for as long as possible. If it doesn't work out for some reason, I know I will be well positioned for a telecommuting job with another firm.

Section Summary

- What stage of recovery do you believe you are in? (Refer to your original answer.)

  I believe I am fluctuating between the "putting the self into action" and "appealing to the self" stages.

- What do you believe is your potential for recovery? Has your answer changed?

  I am confident that I can make significant progress with my recovery. My answer is the same.

- In the time since the most severe period of your illness, what have you achieved in symptom reduction?

  I have regained much of my energy and zest for life. For the most part, I am sleeping better, and I am eating well. I am better able to concentrate and make decisions. Most importantly, I feel that I have value, and I experience joy on a regular basis.

- What have you learned about coping skills for managing the symptoms you still experience?

I have learned that drawing on a variety of coping skills on a consistent basis requires vigilance and energy, but the effort keeps my symptoms in check, and that is priceless. When I start to feel anxious or depressed, my "go-to" coping skill is asking people I trust for support.

- What have you learned about self-acceptance?

   I have learned that self-acceptance and recovery are intertwined, and they require constant work. I have also learned that self-acceptance includes understanding and respecting my limitations and feeling whole, vital, and worthy in spite of them.

- Do you have a different understanding of the losses that have occurred in the time since the initial experience of your mental illness? If so, describe your understanding.

   I think I have come to a crossroads in my understanding. I feel that I can set down the burden of guilt and shame I feel over the losses that have resulted from my anxiety and depression. And looking back, I see that much of what I held so dear— particularly toxic relationships—was really just an extension of my mental illness, and so any loss of that isn't so significant, after all. At the same time, I have come to understand that doing my best to manage my mental illness is my responsibility and will ensure that I don't lose what really matters, and that will support my recovery.

- Have any positive changes occurred in your life as a result of your mental illness? If so, what are they?

   As I previously mentioned, I believe that my mental illness actually helps me show compassion to others who are struggling. Sometimes I believe my life's purpose is to use my experience to help others with mental illness.

- Are you starting to participate in activities that you once enjoyed but gave up because of your mental illness? If so, what are they?

   This summer I made participating in fun activities with friends a priority.

- What new activities have you undertaken in your recovery?

   I get at least two massages a month and see the chiropractor on a regular basis. These activities make me feel pampered.

- What do you need to do to become more self-accepting?

   I need to remember to be gentle with myself.

Skill Area Five
Developing Personal Recovery Goals (page 153)

- Are you ready to work on a life goal? If so, what goal would you like to set?

  Yes. Recently, three opportunities to become involved in suicide prevention again have come my way. I would like to weigh my options and choose only one to pursue.

- How does self-acceptance play a role in reaching this goal?

  I have accepted that pursuing only one of these opportunities rather than all three honors my limitations and allows me to help others in the way that best fits me. This selectiveness increases my chances of success and, in turn, supports my mental health, happiness, and well-being.

- What skills do you have to achieve this goal? What skills will you need?

  I possess a variety of professional skills to reach this goal. I will need to be vigilant about monitoring my mental state, and when I start to feel overwhelmed and anxious and/or depressed, I will need to make an extra effort to be gentle with myself.

- Who can support you in achieving this goal?

  My husband, friends, and therapist can support me in achieving this goal.

- What barriers will you face? How will you overcome them?

  I must deal with the haunting sense that I never have enough time, energy, or focus to manage my work, physical fitness, and home life. I will continue to work with my therapist on coping with this, and I will continue to try to recognize what I can let go of to support my sanity. I will remember the incredible resilience I possess to have survived so much trauma and heartache. And remembering that I completed the considerable task of editing and "working" this workbook in the face of my struggles—that "I can do it"—will help me succeed once again.

Life Purpose Questionnaire Post-Test (page 157)

Vanessa's Life Purpose Questionnaire Post-Test score: 17

End Notes

Introduction

1. Mary E. Copeland, 1995. *Wellness Action Recovery Plan.* [Online]. Available from http://www.mentalhealthrecovery.com (accessed 14 September 2014).

2. Mary G. Rappaport, 1997. *People with Severe Mental Illness Speak Out for the First Time on the Effects of Stigma.* [Online]. Available from http://www.nami.org/Content/ContentGroups/Press_Room1/19971/July_1997/People_With_Severe_Mental_Illness_Speak_Out_For_The_First_Time_In_Study_On_Effects_Of_Stigma.htm (accessed 14 September 2014).

3. Patricia Deegan, "Recovering our sense of value after being labeled mentally ill," *Journal of Psychosocial Nursing,* volume 31, issue no. 4 (1993): pp. 7–11.

4. Nathaniel Branden, *The Six Pillars of Self-Esteem* (New York: Bantam, 1994) pp. 90–104.

5. Paul E. Bleuler, *Dementia Praecox or the Group of Schizophrenias* (Translated by J. Zinkin, New York: International Universities Press, 1950).

6. Sue E. Estroff, "Self, identity, and subjective experiences of schizophrenia: In search of the subject." *Schizophrenia Bulletin,* volume 15, issue no. 2 (1989): pp. 189–96.

7. Heinz L. Ansbacher and Rowena R. Ansbacher, eds., *The Individual Psychology of Alfred Adler* (Oxford, England: Basic Books, Inc., 1964).

8. Harry S. Sullivan, *The Interpersonal Theory of Psychiatry* (Norton: New York, 1953).

9. Carl Rogers, *Client-Centered Therapy* (Cambridge, Massachusetts: The Riverside Press, 1951).

10. R. D. Laing, *The Divided Self: An Existential Study in Sanity and Madness* (Harmondsworth, England: Penguin, 1960).

11. Agnes B. Hatfield and Harriet P. Lefley, *Surviving Mental Illness: Stress, Coping, and Adaptation (*New York: The Guilford Press, 1993).

Life Purpose Questionnaire

12. The "Life Purpose Questionnaire" was developed by R. R. Hutzell, PhD, and Mary Eggert, PhD. R. R. Hutzell and Mary D. Eggert. 1989. *A Workbook to Increase Your Meaningful and Purposeful Goals.* [Online]. Available from http://www.viktorfrankl.org/source/hutzell_workbook_2009.pdf (accessed 15 September 2014).

Nathaniel Branden's Levels of Self-Acceptance

13. Nathaniel Branden, *The Six Pillars of Self-Esteem* (New York: Bantam, 1994) pp. 90–104.

Virginia Satir's Poem on Self-Esteem

14. Virginia Satir, *Self-Esteem* (Berkley, CA: Celestial Arts, 1975).

Skill Area Two Factors That Undermine Self-Acceptance

15. Esso Leete, "How I Perceive and Manage My Illness," *Schizophrenia Bulletin,* volume 15, issue no. 2 (1989).

16. John Bradshaw, *Healing the Shame That Binds You* (Florida: Health Communications Inc., 2005).

Skill Area Three Building Healthy Relationships

17. Thomas Harris, *I'm OK—You're OK* (New York: Harper-Row, 1967).

18. Heinz L. Ansbacher and Rowena R. Ansbacher, eds., *The Individual Psychology of Alfred Adler* (Oxford, England: Basic Books, Inc., 1964).

Skill Area Four Self-Acceptance and Recovery

19. Elizabeth Kübler-Ross, *On Death and Dying* (New York: MacMillan Co., 1969).

20. Larry Davidson and John Strauss, "Sense of self in recovery from severe mental illness," *British Journal of Medical Psychology*, volume 65 (1992): pp. 131–45.

21. R.C. Kessler, W.T. Chiu, O. Demle, and E.E. Walters, "Prevalence, Severity, and Comorbidity of Twelve-month DSM-IV Disorders in the National Comorbidity Survey Replication (NCS-R)," *Archives of General Psychiatry*, volume 62, issue no. 6 (2005): pp. 617–27.